KALEIDOSCOPE

KALEIDOSCOPE

REMINISCES
of
THE HON'BLE and the WICKED

R. K. Puri

GYAN

ISBN: 978-81-212-6149-4

Published, 2023

Published by

Gyan Publishing House
5, Ansari Road
Daryaganj, New Delhi-110002
Phone: 011-47034999, 9811692060
www.gyanbooks.com
E-mail: books@gyanbooks.com

Printed at: Gyan Press, Delhi.

DEDICATED

to

My dear parents :

Late Mr Kishen Puri &

Mrs Damyanti Puri

and

My devoted wife :

Late Mrs Uma Puri

Contents

Acknowledgements

I owe the compilation of this chronicle of events and experiences of a personal nature to the endearing and irresistible persuasion of my daughter and son-in-law, Shobha and Vibhas Joshi.

Special thanks to my grand-daughter Aparna Joshi, an author of six books at 20 years of age, for her painstaking efforts in wading through the collection of documents, accumulated by me over eight decades, in shortlisting and selecting topics of significance and their dates of occurrence for inclusion in this chronicle.

Thanks to the motivational support and encouragement extended to me by my valued friends and esteemed colleagues, Lieutenant General (retd.) and former Governor, Nirbhay Sharma, Ambassador Kamal Bakshi, Dr. D P Pande, Chief Medical Director, IRHS (retd.) Mrs Lata Singh IAS (retd.), Mr Srinivas Adige IAS (retd.) and Mrs Sudha Kothari, Director Tourism (retd.) that I undertook this task.

My special thanks to two of my valued and affectionate friends of long standing: Ann Morrow, Biographer of British Royalty, former journalist of The Daily Telegraph and renowned author of the 'Highness, the Maharajah's of India'; Lindsay Hebberd, celebrated American photographer and publisher of several coffee table books including the 'Cultural Portraits of India' for their expert advice and encouragement in writing this book.

At this juncture, I specially recall my childhood friend Raj Puri who migrated to USA many years ago. During his annual visits to India, he would spend hours listening to my narrations and encourage me to compile this chronicle.

Last, but not the least, my profuse thanks to Mr Atiq Ahmed for cheerfully applying his professional skills in entering my handwritten articles on the computer, which greatly facilitated me.

R K Puri

Preface

This is neither my 'autography' nor 'memoirs' but simply a chronicle of events, experiences and vignettes of a personal nature collected by me during six decades of an active service career in the Central Government and the Corporate Sector.

It is a record of fascinating events of pre and post-independent India, I had the opportunity of being associated with, and a collection of enthralling anecdotes of princely states, which constitute the sum and substance of this chronicle.

R K Puri

Prologue

On 14th August 1947, near midnight, Jawahar Lal Nehru, the first Prime Minister of India, began his historic ***"Tryst with Destiny"*** speech in India's Parliament thus:

> "Long years ago, we made a tryst with destiny, and now the time comes when we shall redeem our pledge .... At the stroke of the midnight hour when the world sleeps, India will awake to life and freedom.........................."

It is regarded as the greatest speech of the twentieth century.

I met the great man twice, once as a student to secure his autograph, the second time as an Indian Police Service Officer in a meeting at his official residence.

On 17th January 1950, Field Marshal K M Cariappa, First Commander-in-Chief of Indian Army, inscribed a piece of advice in his autograph :

> "Do not speak ill of another person unless you are certain of facts and figures, even if you are, say to yourself why speak?"

Twenty-one years later in 1971, the octogenarian Field Marshal and I chanced to meet again, when he enquired if I had followed his advice in my career in the Civil Services.

On 13th December 1971, the tenth day of the Indo-Pakistan war, the Chief of Indian Army, General Sam Manekshaw, issued an ultimatum to General A K Niazi, Commander of all Pak army forces in East Pakistan to:

"SURRENDER OR WE WIPE YOU OUT"

Niazi surrendered, with 93,000 Pak Army troops, on 16th December 1971. The war was over in 13 days. Pakistan lost half its territory, and a new country, Bangladesh, was created.

I was an eyewitness to these historic moments as a representative of the Railway's at the Army Headquarters, to organise the rail transportation of Indian Army troops to two war fronts, East and North and movement of 93,000 Prisoners of War to POW Camps and till their final repatriation at the Wagah border, Amritsar, Punjab.

The Kaleidoscope of the ***"Reminisces of the Hon'ble and the Wicked"*** presents myriads of my experiences of meeting and interacting with global celebrities whose place in the history of their countries is assured.

They include Lord Louis Mountbatten, Field Marshal Edwin Bramall, Prince Charles, Prime Ministers Lord Clement Atlee (UK), Jack Lynch (Ireland), Bandaranaike (Sri Lanka), and numerous other celebrities and Maharajas, many of whom were nation builders, while several amongst them were more focused on activities of leisure, reckless destruction of wildlife, profligacy and debauchery.

At home in India, I had the honour of interacting with several Heads of State: President Dr. Rajendra Prasad, President V V Giri, President Fakhruddin Ali Ahmed, President Sanjeeva Reddy and Prime Minister Narasimha Rao.

ROYALS OF RAJPUTANA

There were 22 hereditary rulers of States in Northwest India, spread over 343,328 sq.kms.

They claimed descent from the Sun, the Moon and various astral lineages, enjoying supreme powers over their subjects.

Some were Honourable Rulers, a few were Wicked!

THE HON'BLE ONE'S

Not all Royals were playboys or spendthrifts. There were the honourable ones who contributed to the upliftment of their subjects.

The Maharajas of larger states of Rajputana like Bikaner, Jodhpur, Jaipur and Udaipur were far sighted and benevolent rulers. They built roads and highways, hospitals and schools, developed industries and factories, provided water and electricity in remote villages and created administrative and legislative infrastructure.

Maharaja Ganga Singh of Bikaner created an irrigation system, the Ganga Canal, in the early 20th century bringing water from Punjab to Ganganagar, to irrigate the region.

Maharaja Umaid Singh of Jodhpur built hospitals, schools and established an airport at Jodhpur putting it on India's air map.

Maharaja Sawai Man Singh of Jaipur developed Jaipur as the **"PINK CITY"** of India, making it a 'must visit' city on the tourist map. He was a very far-sighted prince who dotted Jaipur with colleges, schools, and parks.

An internationally acclaimed polo player, he also served as India's Ambassador to Spain.

Maharana Bhupal Singh of Udaipur was the first Indian prince to sign the Instrument of Accession of his state to the Union of India on 18th April 1948. He rose to become the Maharajpramukh of the new State of Rajasthan.

THE WICKED RULERS

The British rulers of India won them over in an alliance, under which they recognised the suzerainty of the British Crown in return for being allowed unbridled rule of their respective states.

The British rulers also lured the princes to their way of life, rewarding them with titles, and offering facilities of luxury cars, aeroplanes, railway systems in their states, entitling them to a certain number of gun salutes according to the size of their State, and sending them to England on occasions like the King's birthday and offering Convent Schools for the education of their princes.

The rulers were quick to adopt to the British way of life. The results were not always as expected.

STAR OF INDIA

The Viceroy of India, George Nathaniel Curzon, planned a dazzling coronation of King George-V and his Queen at the Delhi Durbar in 1911. He invited all princely rulers of India to attend the installation of King George as the Emperor of India.

He decided to confer the most coveted British honour of GCSI (Grand Commander of the Star of India) to a ruler of a large princely State. The ruler, however, declined the honour as being a descendent of the Sun God, he could not be demoted to a star!

PRINCE 'X'

Maharaja Hari Singh of Kashmir went to London as a Prince in 1919. He became the victim of a blackmail. A British girl by the name of Maudie Robinson met the Maharaja at a ball and trapped him in a most audacious blackmail. The Prince had to sign two cheques of the value of £150 million each. The case was tried in a British Court, where in he was referred to as Prince 'X'. The case as expected, attracted worldwide attention.

Many of the Princes became accustomed to annual holidays abroad with their families and bought costly mansions for their stay. Their sons were educated in Britain, several of them married British and European girls from lower economic and social strata, splurging their State's wealth on buying them expensive gifts of jewellery and salacious houses.

THE WICKED ONES

Some of the rulers built Hunting Lodges in forests for their Viceregal guests to stay and hunt wildlife.

The hunters would perch themselves on "Machaans" (platforms) high up on trees, near the lakes, where tigers and other wildlife would often come to drink water.

A live 'bait' would be kept tied to a tree to tempt the tigers to feed on them. The princes even compelled groups of villagers to enter the forests, beating drums to drive out the wildlife and the shooters would take aim. They would then proudly pose for photographs, holding a gun in hand and their foot on the kill.

Bharatpur's Maharaja organised annual duck shoots for the Viceroys at the famous Keoladeo Bird Sanctuary which attracts over 350 migratory species of birds during winter.

Lord Linlithgow, Viceroy of India, visited along with his friends on 12th November 1938 and shot over 4273 birds in a single day. Linlithgow is believed to have shot around 2000 of them.

A large stone plaque at the Keoladeo National Park displays the dates of various bird shoots, names of Viceroys who shot them and the number of birds killed. A shameful testimony to mindless destruction of wildlife.

These and several other anecdotes of the Hon'ble and the Wicked appear in fuller details in the Kaleidoscope.

1

Royal Rajputana

At the time of transfer of power in August 1947, the British ruled India with two administrative systems namely: British India and Princely India.

British India consisted of 11 provinces, namely, Madras, Bombay, Bengal, United Provinces (UP), Punjab, Bihar, Central Provinces (CP), Assam, Orissa, Sind and North West Frontier Province (NWFP), each ruled by a Governor, appointed by the Viceroy.

Princely India consisted of 565 States, each governed by a hereditary Ruler under the suzerainty of the British Crown administered by a subsidiary alliance. Of these, 22 Princely States of north - west India, known as, ***Rajputana***, were under the political control of an Agent to the Governor General (AGG). His headquarter was established at Mount Abu, situated on a high plateau in the Aravalli Range, which offered a cool and inviting climate to the British expatriates serving in these States to spend the summer there with their families. Mount Abu, soon developed as a popular hill resort.

Princely states had internal autonomy while the Rajputana Agency (under the AGG) was responsible for the external affairs of the states.

The Maharajas, soon followed the Britishers and built palatial houses on the higher peaks, where they could socialise with the Agent and other high officials of the British Empire.

The British very adroitly pandered to their heightened sense of rule by divine right and glory by granting them the privilege of varying number of gun salutes on special occasions like their birthdays or when visiting the Viceroy in Delhi. The gun salutes varied from 3 for smaller states to 21 gun salutes for the larger states in recognition of their status.

To emphasise higher status, the Viceroy was entitled to a 31 gun salute while the King Emperor would receive a 101 gun salute.

In addition to these privileges, the British instituted high sounding awards like the Grand Commander of the most noble Victorian Order (GCVO), and the Grand Commander of the Star of India (GCSI). The awards were announced on the King's birthday or on New Year's Day.

Occasionally, the awards were declined by a princely ruler on the ground that being a descendant of the Sun God, he could not accept an award which lowered his status to a Star.

The awards were conferred to them by the Viceroy at ceremonial functions with much fanfare and gun salutes.

The British rulers encouraged the Indian rulers to send their princes for education to Harrow or Eton, Cambridge or Oxford. The rulers were invited to visit London to felicitate His Majesty the King on his birthdays, play polo with the British royals and dress in latest style of suits made by tailors of Bond Street and Saville Row.

Pampered by their British Residents, the Princes became westernised, aped their customs, acquired fleet of luxury vehicles like the Rolls Royce, Cadillacs and other sports cars.

In India, they built luxurious Palaces patterned on Versailles or Scottish Castles and constructed hunting lodges in forests where they could invite the Viceroys and British Governors to participate in hunts. In their desire to please the British rulers, they became divorced from their people.

Some of the Princes developed strange notions of their affinity with the British Crown. One of the Ruler's of a smaller state even conveyed his blessing to King Edward VIII and his American wife Mrs Simpson! The ruler of one of the largest states of Rajputana used to sign off his letters to King George V as the most obedient servant of Your Imperial Majesty, copies of which are on display in the photo gallery at the Hotel Imperial, New Delhi.

Some of the rulers of Princely States who considered it infra-dig to accept an award of the Grand Commander of the Star of India (GCSI) as demeaning of their high pedigree as descendants of the Sun God, however, deemed it an honour to be appointed an honorary Aide-de-Camp (ADC) of the His Majesty the King Emperor.

The princely rulers had immense faith and confidence in Lord Mountbatten's strong support for them. They considered him as one of their own. Some of them hosted him lavishly at their states and he enjoyed shooting tigers at hunts organised by them. A few of them even called him Dicky and played Polo with him.

On 25th July 1947, the Rulers assembled in Delhi for a meeting with their Viceroy, Dicky. It was a very sombre Lord Mountbatten who addressed them. His message was simple. India was moving close to independence. The Princes must make their peace with political leaders– Gandhi, Nehru or Jinnah and decide whether they wished to be integrated with India or Pakistan before 15th August 1947.

After Mountbatten had spoken, the Princes began to ask about their rights to retain their privileges, their palaces, their gun salutes etc. Mountbatten found their questions as a moment of the greatest historical change in the sub-continent rather appalling and incredibly childish.

On 14th August 1947 ***"at the stroke of midnight,"*** a new nation India was born. It signalled the end of the British era in India and that, of the Princely Rule in Rajputana.

PART - I
Resurgent Rajasthan

2

Resurgent Rajasthan

With the shutting down of the Rajputana Agency on 14th August 1947, all treaties and alliances of suzerainty of the British Crown over the Princely States of Rajputana stood abrogated.

The twenty-two princely states of Rajputana were declared annexed to the new state of Rajasthan.

The Princes of the larger states of Bikaner, Jodhpur, Jaipur and Udaipur agreed to accede to the Union of India. The smaller princes felt powerless and abandoned by their British friends.

The process of merger of the princely states of Rajasthan had begun.

Sardar Vallabhbhai Patel, the Home Minister of India, a seasoned politician presided over the relations with the princes. He was determined to ensure accession of every prince to the new state but was mindful of the sensitiveness of the princes and about their respective status in the echelons of the hierarchical systems of the royalty.

Maharana Bhupal Singh of Udaipur was the most senior Royal of Rajasthan, claiming descent from the Sun God. He was, however, paralytic from his childhood and could not be burdened with any executive responsibilities. Sardar Patel bestowed on him the rank of "Maharajpramukh" of Rajasthan. In the warrant of precedence, he ranked above Governors of States, and the highest rank for any prince in India. It satisfied the Maharana.

Next in seniority among the royals, Sardar Patel appointed Maharaja Sawai Man Singh of Jaipur, an internationally acclaimed sportsman and celebrated polo player, as the Rajpramukh of Rajasthan, with the executive powers of a Head of State. He held the office from 1st July 1949 to 31st October 1956.

Maharaja Bhim Singh of Kota, was appointed the Uprajpramukh of Rajasthan. He was officiated as Rajpramukh of the State in the absence of Maharaja Sawai Man Singh from the country.

Jaipur, being the largest city of Rajasthan was declared the capital of the new formed state.

The three most popular leaders of the freedom struggle in the state were elected as the Chief Minister of the new State:

(i) Mr Hira Lal Shastri	:	1949-51
(ii) Mr Jai Narain Vyas	:	1951-54
(iii) Mr Mohan Lal Sukhadia	:	1954-71

The state was divided into the following 5 Divisions for all administrative and law and order purposes :

(i) Udaipur Division
(ii) Jaipur Division
(iii) Jodhpur Division
(iv) Bikaner Division
(v) Kota Division

Each Division was headed by a Divisional Commissioner. The Districts headed by collectors were also included in those divisions. In total there were 33 Districts in the new state.

My father, Mr Kishen Puri, being the seniormost officer in the state, was appointed the:

(i) Commissioner of Udaipur	:	1949 - 1951
(ii) Commissioner of Jaipur	:	1951 - 1953
(iii) Chief Secretary of the State	:	1953 - 1957

As the Chief Secretary of the new State, Mr. Kishen Puri negotiated the merger of Mount Abu from the Bombay province with Rajasthan in 1954 and of the independent province of Ajmer in Rajasthan in 1956.

With the merger of these two provinces, the process of merger of princely states which began on 15th August 1947 and their unification into the new state of Rajasthan was completed in 1956.

This was followed by the enforcement of the States Reorganisation Act on 1st November 1956 synchronising with the Constitution Amendment Act, 1956 which restructured the framework of the states of India on a linguistic basis.

Rajasthan, enlarged by the addition of Ajmer and Mount Abu, attained an equivalent status as a state. The Rajpramukh of Rajasthan Maharaja Sawai Man Singh of Jaipur demitted his office on 31st October 1956, and the same was followed by the Maharana of Udaipur as "Maharajpramukh" and Maharaja of Kota as "Uprajpramukh".

Mr Kishen Puri welcoming the Union Home Minister of India Govind Vallabh Pant and Sardar Gurmukh Nihal Singh, Governor of Rajasthan.

Sardar Gurmukh Nihal Singh was appointed the first Governor of Rajasthan. He held the office from 1st November 1956 to 15th April 1962.

Mr Mohan Lal Sukhadia continued as the first Chief Minister of the new state of Rajasthan.

My father, Mr Kishen Puri continued as the first IAS Chief Secretary of the new state of Rajasthan till his retirement in 1957.

3

The Viceroys' Wicked Hunt

British nobility has a long standing tradition of participating in hunts for pheasants, grouse and foxes. In India, the Viceroys and Army officers took to big game hunting like tiger hunts, pig sticking and bird shooting.

The sport provided an avenue for upward mobility for the British army soldiers and subalterns in India to upstage hunting performances for the nobility.

The rulers of princely states in India were quick to recognise the potential of cultivating the Viceroys and high ranking British officials by inviting them to elaborate hunting expeditions to their states and territories.

Tiger hunts and bird shooting became standard recreations for British officials and their wives. The rulers developed, and earmarked game reserves, building palaces for the stay of their guests.

In 1911, King George-V and his retinue, after the Coronation ceremony in Delhi, killed 39 tigers.

During the tiger hunts, the British officials would perch themselves high up on the trees in the safety of 'Machaans' and the tigers would be drawn out from their lairs by local drum beaters moving on foot in the forests. Some Maharajas invited their guests to ride on elephants for hunting the tigers. The Britishers would pose for photographs with the kill, gun in hand and one leg on the dead animal.

India's tiger population was nearly decimated as around 80,000 tigers were killed between 1875 and 1925.

Lord Curzon, the Viceroy of India, accompanied by Field Marshal Lord Kitchner, Commander-in-Chief of the British Indian Army inaugurated the Keoladeo National Park of Bharatpur located between two of India's top tourist cities, Jaipur and Agra on December 1, 1902 by shooting birds with his party of friends and family. They killed 540 birds on a single day.

The next Viceroy to visit this world famous bird sanctuary was Lord Linlithgo accompanied by his party of 50 guns. They shot 1415 ducks on a single day on 9th November 1936. A marble slab stands prominently at the entrance of the bird sanctuary, with the names of Lord Linlithgow and his party of 50 guns displayed on it along with their kill of 1415 birds on a single day.

This merciless and senseless killing of birds whetted Lord Linlithgow's appetite and he returned thereafter on three more occasions to improve his tally of bird killing:

(i) December 6, 1936 with 41 guns. They shot 1476 birds;
(ii) February 6, 1937 with 35 guns. They shot 2568 ducks;
(iii) December 12, 1938 with 39 guns. They killed 4273 innocent ducks on a single day.

Another famous wildlife game sanctuary is the Gajner Sanctuary, which has an abundance of deer, desert foxes and wild boars. During the British era, the ruler of Bikaner had built a Palace for the stay of Viceroys and Princes invited for the hunts there.

Lord Elgin and Lord Irwin, Viceroys of India, and the Prince of Wales were among the British Royals who visited this Sanctuary for hunting Imperial Sandgrouse.

Even after the Independence of India, Queen Elizabeth and the Duke of Edinburgh during their visit to India in 1961 took part in a controversial tiger hunt at Ranthambore Wild Life Reserve. The Duke of Edinburgh killed an 8 ft. tiger during the 3-day hunt.

4

Royal Capers

During British rule in India from 1847 to 1947, Mount Abu located at a height of 5650 ft. in the Aravalli range was the political headquarter of the Rajputana Agency headed by an Agent of the Governor - General of India (AGG).

It soon became the summer resort of a large community of British expatriates and their families based in the princely states of Rajputana and other Provinces under the British rule.

Their influx gave a boost to the construction of private bungalows, Scottish style cottages, clubs, convent schools and churches, even a large Polo Ground was constructed in the centre of the city.

Mount Abu soon began to be dotted with magnificent palaces of the Princely Rulers of the states of Rajputana. They had entered into alliances with the British rulers, accepting the suzerainty of the British Crown, and were therefore under the political control of the Agent to the Governor General of India.

They lived in their palaces with large retinues of staff and hosted lavish parties to cultivate their rapport with the AGG and other high ranking British Officials.

Mount Abu being a small town with a small number of commercial establishments and the overcrowding by Indian visitors and large retinues of the Royal families, the need was felt for regulation of pedestrian traffic, cycles, cars and rickshaws pulled by coolies, on the Mall Road.

The civic authorities issued public notices banning movement of vehicular traffic, local pedestrians, hawkers and rickshaws pulled by coolies and dogs on the Mall Road.

Exceptions were made in respect to the flag cars of the Agent to the Governor General, privately owned rickshaws pulled by uniformed and licenced coolies. Dogs accompanying their owners on leash were allowed.

Most of the rulers of the states residing in their palaces at Mount Abu accepted the new regulations gracefully, the only exception being the ruler of a small state who had also built a palace in the hill station. He decided to teach the Britishers a lesson or two.

As privately owned rickshaws were allowed, he arranged for his dogs to be sent out on the Mall Road in his monogrammed rickshaws, pulled by his uniformed orderlies.

The British housewives on their outing with their pet dogs, in privately owned rickshaws, could not match the opulence of the Maharajas dogs in their finery, riding in the rickshaws bearing royal monograms. They felt slighted and insignificant by comparison.

The next day notices appeared banning all dogs on the Mall Road, it applied to the Maharaja's dogs as well.

The Maharaja came up with another strategy. He sent his staff to Abu Road town, 20 km away, which supplied all household items needed by the residents of Mount Abu, to procure two or three car loads of stray dogs at night and release them on the Mall Road. Next morning Mount Abu woke up to see the sight of the four traffic policemen on duty on the Mall Road, chasing the dogs who would scamper up the hill side or slide down and escape. It was an unequal chase and the dogs could not be cornered.

The next day, the Maharaja thought of getting the entire supply of fresh food including bread, butter, eggs and milk to be bought by his staff and distributed to the poor and destitutes of Abu Road. In the morning, the residents woke up to the tantrums of their children deprived of their breakfast; the seniors having to begin their day sans their ***"chotta hazri"***, and staple of bread and eggs.

The culprit was discovered and expelled from Mount Abu. He never returned to it in his life time.

5

The Coronation of a Maharaja

An Indian prince, upon succession to the throne of his state in Rajputana decided to hold his coronation on a grand scale.

He invited a large number of dignitaries including the Maharajas of various Princely states, British Governors of States, Generals to attend the function. A special invitation was extended to the then Commander-in-Chief of the British Indian Army, Field Marshal Birdwood and his family, having met them earlier at Shimla.

Lord Birdwood has described this esoteric event in India of the early 20th century in his autobiography ***"Khaki and Gown"*** in graphic detail as reproduced below:

"The Maharaja proved himself a wonderful stage manager and arranged a display that can rarely be seen. He arrived in a specially made carriage, drawn by ten elephants. A dozen of his Chief Sardars (Thakurs), all beautifully attired, squatted on a platform facing the Maharaja, who was covered with jewels and enthroned in state. The Durbar was held in a great open court.

The Maharaja was seated on a white platform, wearing a Gold crown. A salute of 101 guns was fired and the whole place broke out in illumination.

A green light converged on the central figure who sat motionless throughout the ceremony. I think he really felt at that moment he was a reincarnation of the God Krishna".

Lord Birdwood was accompanied by his daughter Judith and her friend, an English girl who shared her tent.

Describing the piece-de-resistance in ensuring the comforts of the high ranking guests invited for the royal ceremony, Lord Birdwood stated that ***"the Maharaja had a large and luxurious camp pitched for the accommodation of his eminent guest invited for the ceremony"***.

Attached to each tent was a small bath tent, having a bathtub with a rather strange contraption for an overhead shower which released the water upon pulling a rope.

When his daughter Judith's friend was taking her bath, she pulled the rope designed to release the water whereupon to her great shock and consternation, an obsequious voice asked from above "if the Missy standing other end of the bath, I putting water on her". Missy baba did not know where to hide for cover!.

6

Banquet for the Viceroy

During their visit to Udaipur in 1932, Lord Willingdon, Viceroy of India and Lady Willingdon stayed at the magnificent Jagmandir Palace on Lake Pichhola.

They visited the various historic palaces of Udaipur including the Chittor Fort, the Jaisamand Lake, the historic battleground of Haldighati and the Wildlife sanctuaries of Sajjangarh and Kumbalgarh.

On the day before their departure, the Maharana of Udaipur hosted a banquet for them at the famed Laxmi Vilas Palace perched on top of a hill overlooking the Fatehsagar Lake.

As per plan, the host Maharana Bhupal Singh was to reach the banquet venue of Laxmi Vilas Palace, accompanied by two busloads of his Thakurs, (courtiers) half an hour before the Guest of Honour, Lord Willingdon and his entourage were to arrive.

The accompanying Courtiers dressed in their formal Sherwani (Long coats) with turbans, medals and swords dangling from their scabbards, as per their custom, shed their footwear outside the reception hall.

The Master of the ceremony, the Military Secretary of the Maharana holding the hand of a Major General emerged from the Banquet Hall to check the arrangements at the entrance foyer for the 'welcome on arrival' ceremony.

The General was nearly struck by apoplexy, as he gazed at the vast spread of footwear of all shapes and sizes spread all over the ceremonial platform where the Viceroy was to alight from his open top Rolls Royce.

On hearing the siren it was a do or die situation as by now the siren sounded at a closer distance, the General sprang to action. Looking round for help he spotted a tall, well-built gardener tending the flower bed on the front side. He snapped angrily at the gardener ordering him to remove the footwear littering the reception area.

The tall fellow gave him an angry look of resentment at being asked to do this lowly task. As the siren sounded from a close distance, the gardener piled the shoes in his cart and wheeled them away.

The General heaved a sigh of relief and sprang to welcome their Excellencies, as they made a ceremonial entry in the Banquet Hall. The crisis had been averted and the honour of the host saved.

The next day, the Viceroy hosted the return reception for his host Maharana and his high ranking officials. The Maharana's Military Secretary, now in a relaxed mood, was moving among the guests, greeting them.

The General met the Viceroy's Military Secretary, a tall British Brigadier wearing his ceremonial uniform and medals. The two exchanged pleasantries. A few minutes later, the Brigadier smilingly asked the host General if he had done a good last minute job of removing the hoard of shoes at the previous day's reception.

The Rana's Military Secretary stood stunned, completely speechless, as it dawned on him that the gardener of the previous evening was none other than the British Brigadier in disguise, keeping an eye on the security arrangements for the Viceroy!

The Maharana's Military Secretary dined on this story for a long time, keeping his peers and guests regaled.

7

Cottage that Colonel James Tod Built

My weekends in Udaipur with father were devoted to excursions to historical monuments, forts, old palaces, temple towns of Nathdwara, forts of Chittorgarh and battlefields like Haldighatti and learning about their significance.

One such visit was to a village known as 'Todgarh' situated at a distance of 120 miles from Udaipur to see the derelict house of an Englishman, James Tod who lived there from 1818 to 1822.

The excursion was undertaken to acquaint me with the work of a celebrated historian whose magnum opus, "The Annals and Antiquities of Rajasthan", written in two volumes and published in 1829 remains the most authentic chronicle of The Rajput ever written.

James Tod came out to India at the age of 17 years in 1799 and joined the East India Company as a cadet in the Bengal Army.

During the Anglo-Maratha wars of that era, Tod did useful intelligence work and was soon appointed Political Agent for the Rajputana's princely states, which included Udaipur, Sirohi, Kota and Jodhpur.

The assignment provided him an opportunity to collect Royal genealogies, manuscripts, inscriptions, coins and thus began the study of the Rajputs.

He wrote about the Rajputs as the bravest, noblest and most valorous people. They claimed their lineage from a complex clan system based on tribal expansionism and the colonisation of unchartered regions. Historians point out that they claimed legitimacy being ***"Chandravanshis' and Suryavanshis"*** descendants of the Moon and the Sun.

The rulers of the princely states of Rajputana expressed high appreciation for his work. This led to suspicion among the East India Company bosses of corruption by Tod and his removal from Rajputana. Tod resigned from the service of the East India Company and returned to England.

The two standing memorials to his memory are the house he built in 'Todgarh' and the "Todgarh Raoli Wildlife Sanctuary' spread over Ajmer, Pali and Rajsamand districts of Rajasthan State covering over 495 sq. kms. of forests. Its main wildlife includes leopards, wild boar, chinkara and wolf.

I was given a tour of the derelict and abandoned house of Colonel James Tod at Todgarh with father pointing out the areas which could have served as his sitting room, study room, dining room, verandahs etc. and the stables for horses, if he had owned any, and stressing how, in the absence of electricity in that era, he must have written his magnum opus, '*Annals and Antiquities of Rajputana*', under the flickering light of a candle or an oil lamp.

Eight decades later, I conclude this account of visiting the forlorn abode of a historian of the nineteenth century with a quotation from his classic book "Annals and Antiquities of the Rajputana", which I can still recall:

> "The name of a woman had to be taken with respect before a Rajput or the sword will spring out of its scabbard".

8

General Cariappa's Unforgettable Advice

General K.M. Cariappa was appointed as the first Commander-in-Chief of the Indian Army on 15th January1949. This day is celebrated in India as the **"Army Day"**.

I had the opportunity of meeting him on two occasions, first time in 1950 as a 12-year-old schoolboy to seek his autograph and the second time as a 33-year-old Railway Officer in 1971 on deputation to the Army Headquarters. The General had a phenomenal memory and recalled both the occasions.

General Cariappa visited Udaipur on 17th January 1950. My father was the first Commissioner of Udaipur Division and hosted a reception in his honour attended by local dignitaries, senior officials and army officers of the area led by Major General U.C. Dubey, GOC, Rajasthan and Delhi Area.

I was then 12 years old and keen to obtain the autograph of General Cariappa. My father introduced me to the General who graciously agreed to my request and inscribed the following advice in my autograph book:

"Do not speak ill of another person,
Unless you are certain of facts
and figures,
Even if you are, say to yourself,
Why speak?"

K. M. Cariappa

17th December 1950
Udaipur

The General then made me sit by his side on the sofa and asked me to read aloud what he had written in my autograph book. I read it somewhat nervously, overawed by his towering presence. He was over 6' 2" tall.

He then explained very calmly the content of his advice inscribed in my autograph book and expressed the hope that I would abide by it all my life.

Twenty-one years later in 1971, I was deputed by the Ministry of Railways to the Army Headquarters as Joint Director of Rail Movements (JDRM) in its Directorate of Movements to plan, organise and implement all rail transportation requirements of the movement of army links and their armaments to the war zones on the Eastern and Western fronts.

I received a call from Lieut. General Sarkar, Quarter Master to contact General K.M. Cariappa at Mysore Bhawan where he was staying in Delhi and assist him in resolving some difficulty in the reservation of his rail accommodation for his return to Bangalore.

I contacted General Cariappa on telephone and obtained the details of his rail reservation requirements, which I got resolved and informed him the same day. The old General was profusely thankful for my help.

I then reminded him of the valuable advice he inscribed in my autograph book in 1950. It aroused his curiosity and he asked me if I remembered what he had written in my book and if I could recall its first few words.

As I reeled off the first line:

"Do not speak ill of another person", he stopped me half way and himself recited the remaining three lines of his inscription in my autograph book twenty-one years ago.

He then went on to ask me if I had been following his advice, which I confirmed tongue-in-cheek.

It made me marvel at the exceptional calibre and class of the old Generals who led the armies and brought honour to their country.

General Cariappa had retired on 14th January 1953 and came out to exhort and inspire the Indian Army in the 1965 Indo-Pak war in which his son, Squadron Leader K C Cariappa's aircraft was shot down and he was made a Prisoner of War (POW) by Pakistan.

General Ayub Khan, President of Pakistan, who had served under General Cariappa, called him to say his son was being well treated in Pakistan. The old General told Ayub Khan that all Indian soldiers captured in the war are his sons and they should all be equally well treated.

In January 1986, a grateful nation honoured General Kodandere Madappa Cariappa by conferring on him the highest honorary rank of a Field Marshal.

The facsimile of his autograph, which I have carefully preserved, appears below:

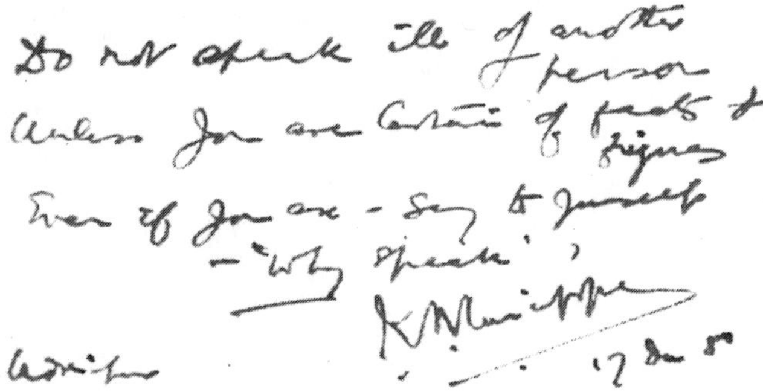

Do not speak ill of another person
unless you are certain of facts & figures
Even if you are - say to yourself
- "Why speak"?

K M Cariappa

9

Sir Donald Field, Last British Satrap of Rajputana

Sir Donald Moyle Field was the longest serving Chief Minister of the princely State of Jodhpur from 1936 to 1945. Prior to that he had served as Chief Minister of the Udaipur state. He was among the last of the British Satraps of the Rajputana Agency to depart from India before its Independence.

The popular Field Club at Udaipur and the summer residence at Mount Abu known as ***"Field Sahab Bungalow"*** bear testimony to his long innings as a British Satrap in Rajputana.

I gathered from my father, Mr Kishen Puri, who was then Chief Secretary of Jodhpur state, the story Field shared with him of his coming out to India at the age of 17 as a rookie in the British Indian Army and being sent to serve in the North West Frontier Province. He found the terrain harsh and inhospitable and its people hostile. This was a phase of his life he rued and returned home.

Destiny and circumstances combined to pull him out of the NWFP and propelled him into the elite Indian Political Service, the 'eyes and ears' of the British Crown in the princely States.

The Political Agents, as they were called, donned white tunics with gold braids and epaulettes, long tailing sabres and 'sola topees', adorned with imperial plumes as they rode in horse drawn 'Buggies' with proper cavalry support, enough to awe the local citizenary and even the princely rulers.

Field's new career in the Indian Political Service took him to the dizzy positions of Resident in Kashmir, Chief Minister of Udaipur and later of Jodhpur for the longest period from 1935-1945.

During this period, Jodhpur was in the thick of India's freedom movement. There were almost daily processions of groups of 'Praja Mandals' (groups of party workers) chanting Mahatma Gandhi's mantra of 'Quit India'. The situation was turning volatile by the day.

At the height of agitation in the state, according to an apocryphal story, an invitation was extended to Pandit Nehru to visit Jodhpur as a state guest by the then Ruler of Jodhpur, Maharaja Umaid Singh, a wise and far-sighted ruler who could read the writing on the wall. There was widespread joy among the people as the news of Nehru's arrival spread.

The preparations for welcoming the second tallest leader of India's freedom movement on his arrival in Jodhpur unnerved Sir Donald Field. He diplomatically remembered a long standing commitment to join his compatriots in a "Shikar" (hunting) expedition in the wilds of Central Provinces (now called Madhya Pradesh) being hosted by the princely rulers of that region.

Prior to his departure for the hunting expedition, Sir Donald left a hand written letter addressed to Mr Nehru with the State's Chief Secretary to personally deliver it to the distinguished guest on his arrival in Jodhpur. In his letter Sir Donald conveyed his profuse disappointment and apologies for not being personally present to welcome him in Jodhpur. He also reminded Nehru of the chance meeting that he and his wife, Carmen, had with him on arrival at a British port.

Nehru took a minute to recall meeting the British couple and smilingly recalled that Carmen used to invariably join a group of the ship's passengers who would surround him on the deck and engage him in long, and animated discussions about India's struggle for freedom from the British Rule.

Carmen would empathise with India's freedom struggle without letting it be known that her husband, an Englishman, was in the active service of the British Rule in India against whom the freedom struggle was being waged. He came to know this fact only later when she introduced Donald Field to him on alighting from the ship at a British port.

Nehru is said to have graciously reciprocated with his good wishes to the British couple and expressed the hope to meet them in happier times in free India.

Field Cottage

Sir Donald and Lady Field left for England in 1946 to retire on his imperial laurels at his country home in England.

The popular 'Field Club' at Udaipur and the 'Field Cottage' at Mount Abu, now a five-star hotel continue to bear testimony to his decade long rule in the princely states of the erstwhile Rajputana.

Farewell letter from Sir Donald Field to my father, Mr Kishen Puri

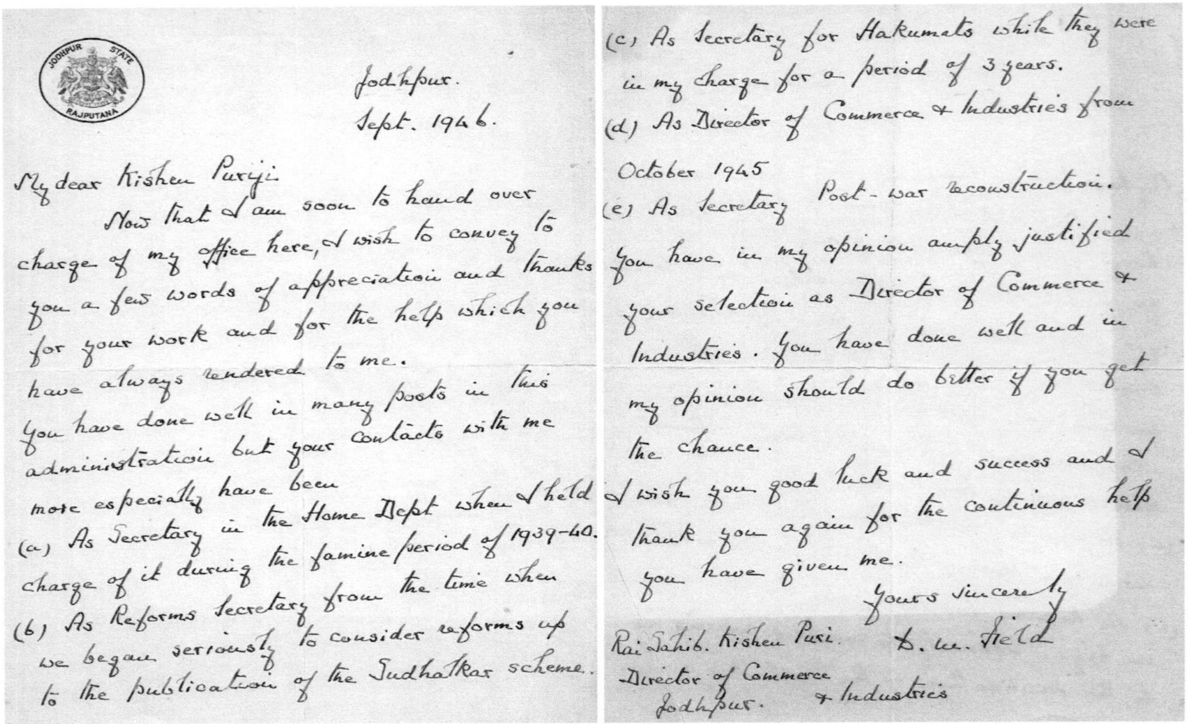

Jodhpur.
Sept. 1946.

My dear Kishen Puriji

Now that I am soon to hand over charge of my office here, I wish to convey to you a few words of appreciation and thanks for your work and for the help which you have always rendered to me.

You have done well in many posts in this administration but your contacts with me have been more especially

(a) As Secretary in the Home Dept when I held charge of it during the famine period of 1939-40.

(b) As Reforms Secretary from the time when we began seriously to consider reforms up to the publication of the Sudhatkar scheme.

(c) As Secretary for Hakumats while they were in my charge for a period of 3 years.

(d) As Director of Commerce & Industries from October 1945

(e) As Secretary Post-war reconstruction.

You have in my opinion amply justified your selection as Director of Commerce & Industries. You have done well and in my opinion should do better if you get the chance.

I wish you good luck and success and I thank you again for the continuous help you have given me.

Yours sincerely
D. M. Field

Rai Sahib. Kishen Puri
Director of Commerce & Industries
Jodhpur.

10

Reminisces of Presidents of India

Dr. Rajendra Prasad

I had the honour at 13 years of age of being introduced to Dr. Rajendra Prasad, First President of the Republic of India on 4th February 1951 at Udaipur and the privilege of securing his autograph.

With President Dr. Rajendra Prasad (1950)
PHOTO OF PRESIDENT ON ARRIVAL AT AIRPORT
being received Mr. Kishen Puri

The President was on a 3-day visit of Udaipur and was staying at the State Guest House, Laxmi Vilas, formerly the Palace of the Maharana of Udaipur, built in 1911, on an elevated platform overlooking the famous Lake Fateh Sagar.

My father, who was Divisional Commissioner of Udaipur had a lengthy session with the President who expressed keen interest in the literature and language of the Mewar region and was curious about the Bardic chronicles of the state and how they inspired the Rulers in their wars against invaders.

The President was quite moved by the tale of a Bard's influence on Maharana Fateh Singh, the ruler of Udaipur's decision not to attend the coronation of King George-V in Delhi in 1911.

The Viceroy of India, Lord Harding was determined to have all Indian Rulers to attend the Delhi Durbar of 1911 and pay their respect by bowing before the King Emperor.

Maharana Fateh Singh, though initially reluctant to attend the Delhi Durbar was eventually persuaded to attend. He decided to travel by a special train with his entourage which included the chief Bard in his court.

According to the tale, the train was halted at a midway station for a short while, when the Rana opened his saloon's door to look at the scenery outside.

At that moment, the accompanying Bard appeared before him and after bowing recited a poem in Dingal language whose English translation was recited by my Father to the President. The poet told the Rana:

"That Lions have lowered their heads,
Jackals are raising their heads and Howling,
Because, O Rana, you have forgotten
the oath of your ancestors"

The Rana was so moved by the Bard's reminder of the oath of his ancestor Maharana Pratap, that he and his descendants would not sleep on beds or be at one place till they re-joined Chittorgarh and threw the invaders (Mughals) out of India, that he did not proceed further towards Delhi and returned to his capital.

President Rajendra Prasad was also moved to know that Gadiya Lohars (Iron Smiths) who had fought under Rana Pratap at Chittorgarh in 1576 have continued to abide by their sacred vow, by neither sleeping at one place nor eating off utensils. With India's Independence, the Gadia Lohars were persuaded to consider themselves as freed from their vow. (Pandit Jawaharlal Nehru held a meeting with them in April 1955 to reassure them of India's Independence and hence they were free from their vow, to abandon their nomadic life).

The next day my father invited a famous Bardic Chronicler to recite his poems recalling the chivalry of Rajput warriors and their women's bravery and sacrifices before the President.

I was introduced to the President at the session along with two other youngsters from the Udaipur Royal family who gracefully agreed for a photograph with us standing behind his chair. The President inscribed his autograph in my autograph book. It remains amongst my cherished autographs:

PHOTOGRAPH WITH THE PRESIDENT

The author can be seen standing second from the left

HON'BLE PRESIDENT V V Giri : 1969-74

Hon'ble President V.V. Giri was the 4th President of India who held office from 24th August 1969 to 24th August 1974. As the President of India, he signed two revolutionary documents: the Shimla Agreement between Mrs Indira Gandhi, Prime Minister of India and Mr Z A Bhutto, Prime Minister of Pakistan, the other, Mrs Gandhi's Bank Nationalisation Bill.

President V V Giri had a long association with the Indian Railways having been the founder Secretary General of the All India Railwaymen's Federation in the early 1930s.

When the Indian Railways hosted the 10th Session of its Railway Committee in New Delhi from 13th November 1969 to 21st November 1969 under the aegis of the United Nations Economic Commission for

Asia and the Pacific (UN-ECAFE), President Giri graciously agreed to host a Reception at the Presidential House for the delegates attending the conference.

I was then working as Deputy Director (ECAFE) in the Railway Board for co-ordination with the ECAFE officials during the session and had the privilege of escorting the delegates to Rashtrapati Bhawan and introducing them to the Hon'ble President Mr V V Giri along with my senior colleague Mr Shahid Ali Khan, Director Planning, Railway Board as seen in the photograph.

Mr Shahid Ali Khan & R K Puri (first from the left) with Hon'ble President V V Giri

HON'BLE PRESIDENT Fakhruddin Ali Ahmed : 1974-77

The President of India, Honourable Mr Fakhruddin Ali Ahmed inscribed his signature on the Instrument of Ratification declaring me to be the Chief Negotiator and Signatory for India on the "First Agreement on Tariff Preferences Among Developing Member Countries of the United Nations Economic and Social Commission for Asia and Pacific" at the signing ceremony to be held at the UN-ESCAP Headquarters, Bangkok on the 31st July 1975.

I had the privilege of being the signatory for India to Asia's First Trade Agreement, also known as the ***"Bangkok Agreement"***, along with the Ministers and Plenipotentiaries of four other countries: Bangladesh, Republic of Korea, Laos and Sri Lanka.

India was unable to depute a Minister for the signing ceremony at Bangkok on 31st July 1975 due to a National Emergency being in force in the country from 25th June 1975 to 21st March 1977.

I was then working as Director (Foreign Trade) in the Ministry of Commerce, the nodal Ministry for UN-ECAFE, and had co-ordinated the participation of the inter-ministerial delegations in the meetings of the original 5 negotiating countries for deciding the quantum of tariff concessions to be exchanged by them. It was decided to authorise me to attend the signing ceremony on 31st July 1975 at Bangkok as the Signatory for India. The Instrument of Ratification of Agreement signed by the President of India in my favour was deposited with UN-ESAFE (now ESCAP) Headquarters.

The Bangkok Agreement's aim was to promote inter-regional trade through the exchange of mutually agreed tariff measures and move forward to liberalisation in investments, services and other trade facilitation measures in the region.

Consequent to these negotiations, the Bangkok Agreement emerged as the First Preferential Trade Agreement (PTA) of the region. It is the only Preferential Trade Agreement that links East and South Asia as well as the two most populous countries in the world, India and China which acceded to the agreement in 2001.

It initially focused on tariff concessions on merchandise trade. It has now moved forward to trade liberalisation in services, investment and track facilitation for improving the economies of the region. The Bangkok Agreement is now renamed an "ASIA PACIFIC TRADE AGREEMENT (APTA)".

The author shaking hands with the Hon President Fakhruddin Ali Ahmed

Hon'ble President of India Sanjeeva Reddy

Iran is the largest supplier of crude oil to India and consequently India has been one of the largest foreign investors in Iran oil. The two countries established diplomatic relations on 15th March 1950.

The two countries set up a joint venture Irano Hind Shipping Co. in 1974. This was followed by the visit of an Iranian Trade Delegation in February 1974 to explore the possibilities of promoting mutual economic development.

The visit of the Iran Trade Delegation was to be followed by the state visit of the King of Iran, Reza Shah Pahlavi.

The Iranian Trade Delegation sought a meeting with the Hon'ble President of India, Mr Sanjeeva Reddy which was duly organised by the Ministry of Commerce.

I was then working as Director, South Asia and East Asia Divisions in the Department of Foreign Trade and was deputed to escort the Iranian Trade Delegation to meet the Hon'ble President. I introduced the members of the Iranian delegation to the Hon'ble President of India Mr Sanjeeva Reddy who graciously interacted with them and expressed keen interest in advancing mutual economic and trade lies between the two countries.

The photograph taken on the occasion with the President is appended below:

The Author Introducing Delegates to the Hon'ble President Sanjeeva Reddy

11

Prime Ministers I Met: Reminisces

I had the opportunity of meeting India's first Prime Minister, Pandit Jawahar Lal Nehru on two unforgettable occasions.

The first time was in April 1954 at the All India Congress Committee's Working Session, held on the sprawling grounds of Mayo College, Ajmer during the summer break. I was then a final year student at Mayo College, scheduled to join the undergraduate course in Rajasthan University at Jaipur.

The second time was in August 1961 as an IPS probationer under training at the National Academy of Administration, Mussoorie along with the probationers of all Central Services. We were in Delhi for attending a traditional meeting with the Prime Minister at his residence.

Sensing an opportunity to secure Pandit Nehru's autograph at the AICC meeting, I tried to reach him at the session venue but could not proceed beyond the reception desk. The volunteers manning the reception desk expressed their inability to allow me to enter the enclosure where the meeting was being held, owing to security restrictions.

At that moment I noticed Madam Vijay Laxmi Pandit walking past the reception desk. I promptly requested her for an autograph. She very graciously took my autograph book, which had only two or three autographs and noticing the blank pages asked me to take Pandit Nehru's autograph first.

I pleaded my inability to reach him owing to stringent security control. Madam Pandit asked me to accompany her. She took me straight to Panditji, introducing me as a Mayo College Alumni seeking his autograph.

Panditji graciously obliged and his autograph remains my most treasured possession. I thanked him and extended my autograph book to Madam Vijay Laxmi Pandit for her autograph, which she gave me immediately.

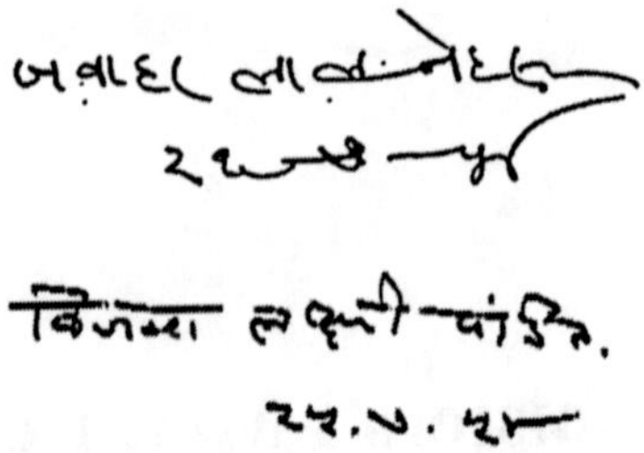

Their autograph came as a windfall for me and spotting. several front line national leaders around Panditji. I managed to secure the autographs of the following leaders:

1. **Mr. Kailash Nath Katju**
2. **Mr. Rafi Ahmed Kidwai**
3. **Mr. Govind Vallabh Pant and**
4. **Mr. V. K. Krishna Menon**

The second meeting with the Prime Minister was the traditional introductory meeting of probationary officers of all Services, IPS, IAS, IFS and Central services, under training at the National Academy of Administration, Mussorie.

The meeting was held at the Prime Minister's official residence, Teen Murti Marg. We were escorted by Brigadier Sheriff, the Deputy Director of the Academy. The probationers were dressed in their formal outfit closed collar coat and trousers.

There were only two chairs in the large hall for the Prime Minister and the Deputy Director and the rest were seated on the carpeted floor. The Foreign Service Probationers were seated nearest to where the Prime Minister and Dy. Director of the Academy sat.

The Prime Minister walked in and was greeted by all of us. The Deputy Director, Brig. Sheriff had seated us in groups of our respective services and each group was introduced to the Prime Minister.

Pandit Nehru briefly addressed the gathering, referring to our role and responsibilities in the service of the nation and dwelt at length on the role of the foreign service officer in projecting the nation's image abroad and fostering the links of friendship and goodwill among nations.

The Prime Minister asked the Foreign Service probationers if any of them knew a foreign language. The probationers kept quiet except one, who raised his hand. The Prime Minister asked him which language he knew.

The probationer answered "English" - the silence that followed in the hall was deafening. The Prime Minister's gaze was fixed on the probationers for a few moments, then he remarked with a bemused smile ***"you think you know"***.

The probationer's response to an acknowledged master of English language, whose ***"Tryst with Destiny"*** speech in English is regarded as the greatest speech of the twentieth century appeared rather churlish.

The meeting ended as the Prime Minister left for the next appointment of his busy schedule.

The reminisce of this meeting with the Prime Minister Pandit Nehru still remains etched in my memory, a half century later.

PRIME MINISTERS OF UK, IRELAND AND SRI LANKA

CLEMENT ATLEE

Lord Clement Atlee served as the Prime Minister of United Kingdom from July 1945 to October 1951. He is remembered in India as the British Prime Minister who announced on 20th February 1947 in the House of Commons the British Government's resolve to grant full self-government to India by 30th June 1948.

The Indian Independence Act 1947 passed by the British Parliament received the Royal Assent on 18th July 1947 and India became Independent on 15th August 1947.

He visited India in 1956 and came to Jaipur, accompanied by Mr Krishna Menon as the Minister in waiting.

With Prime Minister Lord Atlee (1953)
L to R : Lord Atlee talking to Mr Kishen Puri, Chief Secretary Rajasthan. Mr Krishna Menon seated on the extreme left

My father, Mr Kishen Puri, being the Chief Secretary of Rajasthan had a meeting with Lord Atlee along with Mr V K Krishna Menon.

I availed the opportunity to embellish my autograph book with that of Lord Atlee, the political leader responsible for granting freedom to India.

My father, who always had a witty saying up his sleeve shared the following comment made by Winston Churchill on Atlee's role in India's independence in his speech in the House of Commons:

"In the days of Prime Minister William Pitt, never a day went by when the Englishman woke up to read in his newspaper the name of a new country annexed to the British Empire".

"In the no less memorable days of my Right Honourable friend Clement Atlee never a day goes by when an Englishman wakes up to read of the loss of a country by the British Empire".

Winston Churchill also described Clement Atlee on another occasion as a: "Modest little man who has much to be modest about".

PRIME MINISTER SIRIMAVO BANDARANAIKE

In 1974, soon after joining the Ministry of Commerce, Department of Foreign Trade, as Deputy Secretary South Asia Division, I was deputed to attend the last Annual Session of the UN-Economic and Social Commission for Asia and the Pacific (ECAFE) at Colombo.

It was also going to be the first session of an International Organisation in the Chinese built Bandarnaike Memorial Hall of Colombo.

The session was inaugurated by Sirimavo Ratwatte Dias Bandaranaike the world's first lady Prime Minister who served three terms:1960-65, 1970-1977 and 1994-2000.

India had fielded a large delegation of 16 members led by Prof. D.P. Chattopadhyay, Minister of Commerce, and representatives of several other Ministries.

Prime Minister Sirimavo Bandaranaike, graciously spent a few minutes with the Indian Delegation and also posed for a photograph with us:

1975: With Prime Minister Sirimavo Bandarnaike of Sri Lanka at Colombo
Prime Minister Sirimavo Bandarnaike in conversation with a delegate.
The author is seen in the centre

PRIME MINISTER JACK LYNCH OF IRELAND

In the mid-70s, I was deputed to London as Director, Tea Board of India for UK, Ireland and Scandinavian Countries. I served in this capacity from 1977 to 1980.

During my visits to Dublin, I had the opportunity of inviting Prime Minister Jack Lynch to inaugurate a promotional event organised by the Tea Board.

With Prime Minister Jack Lynch, Indian Ambassador
Mr N N Jha, R K Puri and the Lord Mayor of Dublin

12

Indian Police Service 1961 Foundation Course : Mussoorie

On 26th May 1961, the Ministry of Home, Government of India issued my letter of appointment to the Indian Police Service (IPS).

I was directed to report to the Director, National Academy of Police Administration, Mussoorie on 1st June 1961 for attending a residential training programme for 4 months, followed by a one year professional police training programme at the Central Police Training College, Mount Abu.

R K PURI

The National Academy of Administration was established at Mussoorie for training of around 370 Probationers of All India Services like IAS and IPS and the Class I Central Services with the objective of creating awareness of their respective services.

The National Academy of Administration was set up in the premises of the Charleville Hotel located at the end of the Mall Road of Mussoorie.

It was the only hotel in Mussoorie in the beginning of the century where, according to a local legend, Queen Mary of England is believed to have stayed during her visit with King George-V for his Coronation at Delhi Durbar in 1911.

Rudyard Kipling, the well-known Victorian poet, story teller and novelist is reported to have lived there for several years. The Government of India acquired this building for the National Academy of Administration in 1958. Our batch of 1961 was the third one which attended the Foundation course.

I was allotted accommodation Room No. 16 in the main block on sharing basis with an IAS probationer, Dr. Janardan Prasad Singh. He had a distinguished academic record of being awarded Ph.D by the University of London and was admitted to Bar-at-Law by the Middle Temple of Law of London.

We had a very cordial association during the Foundation Course, which continued throughout our service career and into our retired life.

My most memorable recall was of getting to know the Director of the National Academy, Mr Aditya Nath Jha, an ICS officer. He had his residence in the main block of Charleville adjacent to the Lecture Hall.

He was a tall and heavy built person with an imposing presence and would be invariably seated on the lawns of his residence. As the probationers emerged from the Lecture Hall he would invite a few to join him on the vacant chairs around him and engage them in lively conversation, often interspersed by his loud laughter. This was his way of sharing his vast experience with the probationers and also making an assessment of their competence and grasp of the lectures attended by them.

During the Foundation Course from June to October, the Academy invited eminent civil servants, scholars and public figures who interacted with the probationers.

I recall attending an address by a veteran ICS Officer, Sir Chandu Lal Trivedi who shared his experience of the Civil Service Officers during the British rule in India. He was the first Indian Civil Servant to be appointed as the Governor of Orissa by the Viceroy in 1945 and after independence he was appointed as the Governor of Punjab from 1953 to 1957.

The Director Mr A N Jha would occasionally take classes on special subjects like public administration, current events and share anecdotes and stories with the probationers.

I recall an interesting story about Sir Girja Shanker Bajpai, a doyen of the Indian Civil Service, who became a member of the Viceroy's Executive Council in 1946.

In this capacity he was replying to a question raised in the Central Assembly on the appointment of an eminent specialist in the Education Department whose wife was being paid salary for working as his secretary. The questioner asked ***"Is Mrs. X's presence in office a convenience or a necessity ?"***

Sir Girja Shanker's reply to the question was:

"In her capacity as Mr. X's Secretary she is a convenience and as his wife a necessity."

The Assembly dissolved in laughter in which the member who asked the question also joined.

Mr Jha had one more anecdote about Sir Girja Shanker Bajpai to share, with the remark that it has been often related but never confirmed.

According to the anecdote, Sir Girja Shanker Bajpai visited New York to attend an important international meeting. While crossing the 5th Avenue, Sir Girja who was mentally occupied with the complex issue he was to discuss at the meeting, did not notice the traffic light, turning red.

Noticing him crossing the street against the red light, a traffic patrol man shouted to him saying ***"Hey guy you can't cross against the light".***

An offended Sir Girja, pulled himself to his full height and retorted

"I am no guy, I am Sir Girja Shanker Bajpai". The Yankee traffic man yelled back ***"Bajpai or no Bajpai, if you cross the street like that, you will soon be a mince pie".***

The story remains unverified.

13

Central Police Training College, Mount ABU

On completion of our four months Foundation course at the National Academy of Administration, Mussoorie on 31st September 1961, the IPS probationers left for Mount Abu to attend their one-year training at the Central Police Training College before being sent to their respective state cadres to perform their duties as Indian Police Service Officers.

During our training in the Central Police Training College, Mount Abu in 1961, Mr B B Bannerji, IPS was the Commandant, Mr Eric Stracey IPS was the Deputy Commandant and Mr. Davenport was the Assistant Commandant.

Mount Abu was a cool hill station located at a height of 4003 ft. in the Aravali Hills of North West India. The nearest rail head was Abu Road Railway Station at a distance of 20 kms. downhill. Abu Road was the connecting rail head for travellers coming from or going to Delhi or Bombay (now Mumbai).

The Probationary Officers of IPS were required to undergo vigorous physical training from the early morning sounding of Reveille at 5:00 a.m. to what they called dinner parade late night. Few of them had an acronym for that routine i.e. CPTC: "Constant Physical Training Parade".

Six decades is a long span of time to recall the episodes and incidents that occurred during our training phase but a few memories still linger.

Riding on big built mounted police horses was anathema for many of the future Director Generals of Police. Their plight got aggravated when the Riding Instructor would shout to the rider to dismount, remove the saddle and ride bareback.

One such incident stands out. A frisky horse named "Bellaliaka", was a "Hoodoo" of several probationers, especially when called upon to ride the big horse bareback. Some of the riders would even carry pieces of "Gur" (Jaggery) as a peace offering to the brute.

Assistant Commandant Davenport, a retired Irish Sergeant would occasionally come to check the performance of riders. At one such inspection, Davenport noticed one probationer riding bareback was slipping backward on the horse till he fell from its rump on the ground with a thud. Davenport came charging on his horse very close to the fallen rider to enquire "with whose permission did you dismount?" The hapless rider could only mumble "the horse ended".

The Deputy Commandant Mr Eric L Stracy, an IPS Officer of the Tamil Nadu cadre, was a titan among the instructors. He was a model officer, among the senior staff who commanded respect.

A stickler for discipline and etiquette, he took keen interest in the training of officers. He taught them to follow discipline at all times.

He taught them to salute smartly while in uniform. To inculcate this habit in the trainees, he grilled them to follow the procedure of seeking permission to enter his room. If they needed to see him, they had to knock and wait for his response to 'enter'. On entry, they had to focus their eyes on a point marked on the facing wall and march in as on a parade and halt in a circle drawn on the floor, make a smart right turn towards him and salute, holding it for a count of 4, then wait and on being asked to sit, do so gently by not dragging the chair. Take the peak cap-off, but not place it on the office table and keep it on their lap or under the chair.

If any probationer faulted on any of the steps, he would be made to go out and come in following the procedure correctly.

Few of the probationers had reservations about having to salute the Collector, who may be their batch mate, at public functions like Independence Day or Republic Day. They asked a senior guest speaker, a DG level Officer, for advice in such a predicament. He advised them to arrive at the function early and return the greetings of each invitee to the function by a salute. Hence, when the Collector arrives, the salute would not be deemed any different. Eric Stracy, when asked the same question later, told them firmly that they should not in any case feel belittled in saluting a Collector who is the head of the District and authorised to assess the performance of a Superintendent of Police of his district in his Confidential Report.

Mr Stracy was a role model for the probationers of several batches. Post retirement from the Tamil Nadu Cadre, he wrote his autobiography titled ***"The Odd Man Out"***.

He retired as the Director General of Police, Tamil Nadu and later migrated to Australia to join the rest of his family.

PART - II
Switch to Indian Railways

14

Switch to Indian Railway Traffic Service: 1962-1996

On completion of a year's training in the Indian Police Service (IPS) in 1961, I made the switch to the Indian Railway Traffic Service (IRTS) in 1962, on qualifying in that year's All India Civil Services Examination.

It offered me exciting opportunities of working not only in the Railways but in several key Ministries and Central Government Organisations in India and abroad including as a representative of my country in several multilateral conferences convened by United Nations organisations like ECAFE (now ESCAP), UNIDO, FAO, WHO and as Director of India Tea Promotion at London for UK, Ireland and the Scandinavian countries.

In September 1962, when I joined the Indian Railway Traffic Service (IRTS), the service was known by its high-brow name of the ***"Traffic, Transportation and Commercial Department of the Superior Revenue Establishment of Indian Railways"*** till it was reconstituted in 1967 as the IRTS. (Indian Railway Traffic Service)

The service underwent remarkable transformation in the post-independence era graced by the high traditions set for it by the new national leadership.

I recall, even seven decades later, the examples of high ethical traditions set by India's first Prime Minister Jawahar Lal Nehru and the Railway Minister Lal Bahadur Shastri which are etched in my memory.

Among the iconic anecdotes and stories of national leaders who set the traditions of ethical conduct on the Indian Railways after Independence, I recall the one pertaining to India's first Prime Minister Jawahar Lal Nehru.

On 12th February 1948, 13 days after Mahatma Gandhi's assassination, his "ashes" were being taken by a special train to Allahabad for immersion at the Triveni Sangam.

Prime Minister Jawahar Lal Nehru flew to Allahabad to receive the ashes of the Father of the Nation, Mahatma Gandhi and escort them for immersion at the Triveni Sangam.

Allahabad Railway Station was surrounded by unprecedented hordes of people from nearby villages and towns, gathered to pay homage to the departed leader's ashes, making it difficult to enter the station.

The Divisional Superintendent of the Allahabad Railway Division, Mr. Mukherjee, gave very firm instruction to close entry into the main foyer of the Station to ensure smooth passage of the "ashes" on arrival of the train.

Jawahar Lal Nehru's journey from Allahabad airport to the Railway Station was delayed by the milling crowds. The station staff had enforced the 'No Entry' directions firmly and the Prime Minister was prevented from entering the station.

Nehru did not force his way in and patiently waited outside for the ashes to arrive in order to escort them on the boat trip to the immersion point.

After the immersion, Nehru flew back to Delhi. There was much speculation in the Railway circles about the fall out of the action of the Divisional Superintendent in not allowing the Prime Minister's entry into the station.

A week later, the Divisional Superintendent received a letter signed by Prime Minister Nehru expressing his profound appreciation of Mr. Mukherjee's high sense of commitment to duty displayed by his firm directions for enforcement of the "No Entry" rules which ensured the smooth passage of the ashes of the Father of the Nation on such a special and solemn occasion.

Another exceptional example of a Cabinet Minister of the Central Government resigning from his post owning moral responsibility for a disaster in which 112 people were killed was set by Lal Bahadur Shastri, Railway and Transport Minister from 1951 to 1956.

The train accident took place in Mehboobnagar, Andhra Pradesh in August 1956. Shastriji tendered his resignation but was persuaded by Nehru to take it back.

A few months later in November 1956, another railway accident in Ariyalpur in Tamil Nadu resulted in 144 deaths. Shastri promptly submitted his resignation to the Prime Minister Jawahar Lal Nehru and prevailed upon him to accept it on grounds of constitutional propriety. In the last seven decades it remains the solitary example of a Cabinet Minister resigning on grounds of moral responsibility.

During his tenure as Minister of Railways from 1951 to 1956, Lal Bahadur Shastri shunned travel by special trains or in luxurious saloons, instead he preferred to travel by a simple 4 berth First Class Coach setting an example which no other Railway Minister has followed.

The British rulers had created luxurious facilities at Railway Stations and in trains for their exclusive use like Retiring Rooms, First Class Waiting Rooms, Restaurants at stations and dining cars in trains. These were managed by catering contractors who could cater to their culinary requirements. The contractors were awarded titles of Rai Bahadurs in return for their contributions to the War Fund.

Lal Bahadur Shastri abolished all monopolistic catering contracts, rationalised travel facilities on trains, removing restrictions on travel of Indian citizens in First Class Coaches, put an end to "Inter Class" travel in trains which the British had created as an in-between class.

During the Indo-Pak war of 1965, Lal Bahadur Shastri coined the inspiring slogan, "Jai Jawan, Jai Kisan" pasted on all troop trains en-route to the war fronts. It inspired the troops, as masses of citizens chanted this slogan as their trains passed through the stations.

Lal Bahadur Shastri was a true disciple of Mahatma Gandhi, who travelled across the county in the IIIrd Class of trains. Gandhi was once asked why he travelled only by the IIIrd Class to which he responded saying "because there is no IVth Class".

On completing my term of service in the Commercial and Operating Branches of Northern Railway from 1962 to 1968, I was appointed Deputy Director, ECAFE (Economic Commission for Asia and East) the Ministry of Railways to organise the 10th Session of the Railway Committee in coordination with the United Nations – ECAFE at New Delhi. It marked the beginning of my association with UN's Regional Commission in various future projects of national importance for India.

FIVE PHASES OF SERVICE ON DEPUTATIONS

1971 – 73

I was deputed to the Army Headquarters to plan and organise rail transportation of Army's troop movements and armaments to the war zones during 1971 Indo-Pak war and later of the 93,000 Pakistan army soldiers who surrendered to the Indian Army.

1973 – 76

During this period, I served in the Ministry of Commerce as Director

Foreign Trade for South Asia and on 31st July 1975 was appointed Chief Negotiator and Signatory for India in the First Multi-Member Preferential Trade Agreement between Developing member-countries of UN-ESCAP, known as the Bangkok Agreement.

1976 – 79

I was appointed Director of Tea Promotion at London for UK, Ireland and Scandinavian countries.

1980 – 84

On return to India. I was appointed as the Founder Director of Tourism and International Relations Division in the Railway Board and because of my experience and interest, assigned the task of launching a Special Tourist Train for offering facilities of travel to tourist places for the athletes and officials, participating in the 10th Asian Games in Delhi in 1982. I was instrumental in launching India's most famous tourist train known as Palace-on-Wheels which continues to remain the flagship of Indian Tourism.

1984 – 88

During this period, my services were utilised by the India Tourism Development Corporation (ITDC) as Senior Vice President and in this capacity led an 80 member ITDC team to participate in the Festival of India on the Mall at Washington inaugurated jointly by Prime Minister Rajiv Gandhi and President Reagan.

1988 – 90

The Planning Commission appointed me as the Secretary of "National Committee on Tourism" to prepare a long term tourism development Plan for India as directed by Prime Minister Rajiv Gandhi.

1990 – 96

Served as Additional Member Tourism and Catering in the Railway Board and was instrumental in formulating plans for establishment of 100 Hotels on railway sites in India and for establishment of Indian Railways Catering and Tourism Corporation (IRCTC) and developing the "Great Indian Rover" Tourist Train proposal for the Buddhist Sector.

I superannuated from Indian Railways on 30th September 1996.

Details of these proposals and programmes are elaborated later.

15

Indo - Pak War of 1971: Role of Indian Railways - A Ringside View

In January 1971, I was appointed Joint Director MILRAIL in the Army Headquarters. It is a joint unit of the Indian Railways and the Indian Army functioning in the Directorate of Movement of Indian Army.

In April 1971, Prime Minister Mrs Gandhi perturbed by the reports of mass killings by Pakistan Army of Bengali speaking citizens of East Pakistan and exodus of millions of refugees seeking shelter in India held a meeting with the Chiefs of India's Defence Forces, General Sam Manekshaw, Admiral S M Nanda and Air Chief Marshal P C Lal advising them to prepare for intervention in the worsening situation.

The Army Chief General Sam Manekshaw sought six-month time for preparations for a two front war on the Eastern and Western fronts and assured her of victory in a short and swift war. Mrs Gandhi agreed to the Army Chief's request.

General Manekshaw began his preparations for the war immediately. This entailed large scale movement of troops and war material from their bases in various parts of India to the war zones on the Eastern and Western fronts over a distance of 1500 kms.

The MILRAIL unit was tasked to organise running of troop trains to the war zones, preferably by night to avoid dislocation of passengers travelling by day and to avoid panic among the public.

The war began on the evening of **3rd December 1971** with pre-emptive strikes by Pakistan Air Force on eleven Indian airports. The Indian Army responded on 4th December 1971 with a two pronged strategy of defensive operation in the West and offensive war in the East.

Within **ten days** of the commencement of war, the Indian paratroopers surrounded Dhaka on **13th December 1971**. General Manekshaw, Indian

Army Chief sent an ultimatum to Lieut. General AAK Niazi, Commander of Pakistan forces in East Pakistan stating:

"YOU SURRENDER OR WE WIPE YOU OUT"

On 16th December 1971, the thirteenth day of the war, Lieut. General A A K Niazi surrendered with his forces of 93,000 soldiers to Lieut. General J S Arora, General Officer Commanding, Indian Army's Eastern Command at Dhaka. The war ended on the 13th day, the shortest war since World War II.

Following the victory of India in the two front war with Pakistan on 16th December 1971, the QMG (Quarter Master General) Army Headquarters, Lieutenant General Sarkar hosted a celebratory reception at the Defence Service Officers Institute (DSOI), New Delhi to felicitate the Chief Architect of the war, General Sam Manekshaw.

Sam Manekshaw was in a relaxed and cheerful mood. He interacted with all the guests, exchanging a word or two with each invitee and thanking them for the support extended by their organisations in the war effort.

On seeing me with my team of MILRAIL officers staff, he came forward and warmly thanked us for meeting the exacting transportation requirements of the army and armaments to the two fronts in time. He posed for a photograph with us, which has become a treasured memento of our association with India's greatest General.

1971: With Field Marshal Sam Manekshaw at a Bangladesh Victory function
(The author is seen on the left of General Manekshaw)

I was awarded the "VISHIST YOGYATA PADAK" (Distinguished Service Medal) with the following citation :

> ***"Shri R.K. Puri joined the Movement Directorate of the Army Headquarters during the period preceding the national emergency. He got into the thick of the movement operations from the start."***
>
> ***"He displayed unusual skill and confidence in handling military moves by his competent efforts in obtaining willing co-operation from the railway authorities. Between August and December 1971, the Milrail Cell organised the movement of 2000 trains and 30,000 wagons at short notice. Under his direction the Milrail Cell was able to meet these exacting requirements in time and satisfactorily".***

The Ministry of Railways organised a ceremonial function on 15th April 1972, where the Chief Guest, Mr. K Hanumanthaiah, (Union Minister of Railways) bestowed the Vishist Yogyata Medal on me.

Receiving the Medal from Minister Mr. K Hanumanthaiah

16

Moving 93,000 POWs

Our task at the MILRAIL was, however, not yet over. We were required to plan and arrange rail transportation of 93,000 Pakistani Prisoners of War to various POW camps located in various cities, from 1972 to 1973. A special mention needs to be made of the humanitarian concern of General Sam Manekshaw, for the safety, security and treatment of the Prisoners of War in accordance with the Geneva Convention.

General Manekshaw gave specific directions for humanitarian treatment of the Pak POWs in compliance of the Geneva convention in this regard.

The Prisoners of War were to be held in the army camps in various cities in India to ensure their safety and security. These camps were located at the Red Fort in Delhi, Gwalior Fort and at other camps in Bareilly, Meerut, Chandigarh and Amritsar till a decision was taken by the Government on their deportation to Pakistan.

The Army Chief also directed provision of adequate copies of the Quran in the war camps for the POWs who may wish to read their holy book.

General Manekshaw's concern for the treatment of Prisoners of War manifested in an anecdote during his visit to Pakistan after the war. He received a warm welcome from the Pak army units he visited and at Lahore, the Governor of Punjab hosted a lunch in his honour at his residence. After the lunch, the Governor escorted Manekshaw to his car in the portico. The staff at the Governor's residence were standing in a line up by the car to see-off Manekshaw.

The Governor introduced the staff in the line up to the distinguished guest. An old army man in the line-up stepped forward and placed his turban at his feet saying ***"I have five sons in the Pak Army who were taken prisoners of war in India and they had written to inform me that on General Manekshaw's orders, they were given humane treatment and***

even provided copies of Quran in their camps. I, therefore, deem it my duty to pay my respect to you Sir for your kindness to the prisoners of wars".

The MILRAIL Cell in the Movement Directorate of Army HQs completed the transportation of Pak POWs to the war camps in India by 1972 after the signing of the Shimla Agreement by the two Prime Ministers: Mrs Gandhi and Mr Bhutto. The transportation of POWs by trains to Wagah border for their return to Pakistan was completed by August 1972.

Field Marshal Sam Manekshaw was known for his grace and ready wit. Among the numerous instances of his wit, it is relevant to recall the few of his quips in the pre and post 1971 period.

It is said that when Mrs Gandhi asked him if he was ready for military intervention in the situation prevailing in Bangladesh, he is reported to have replied with a firm "No" and added that he had heard BSF, RAW and other paramilitary forces intervening with Mukthi Bahini etc. in Bangladesh but had not been kept advised.

He then assured her that keeping in view Pakistan's likelihood of attacking on two fronts, East and West, and possibility of attack by China, he would require six-months to prepare for military intervention. He assured her of a short and swift war and victory for India.

Mrs Gandhi reposed her full confidence in him and gave her mandate to go ahead with his preparations for war in the winter months.

Recalling his interaction with Mrs Gandhi at his inaugural lecture at the Field Marshal Cariappa Memorial, Manekshaw observed that there is a very thin line between ***"Being made a Field Marshal and being dismissed".***

Another story doing the rounds pertained to a briefing session with Prime Minister Mrs Gandhi attended by Sam along with the Naval and Air Chiefs, Cabinet Secretary and a couple of other Secretaries regarding the operation plan for war with Pakistan.

After the meeting with the Prime Minister, they assembled in Cabinet Secretary's office to review follow up action. The Cabinet Secretary is said to have enquired from Sam ***"Why is it that you always address Mrs Gandhi as Prime Minister, while others address her respectfully as Madam ?"***

Sam's razor sharp response left the bureaucrats speechless:

"Gentlemen, at the school I attended, I was taught that the expression Madam connotes a certain type of lady of leisure and I have much too high regard for Prime Minister to address her by that description".

Following the historic victory of Indian army in the war with Pakistan, Sam related an amusing story of him and Yahya Khan being fellow officers at the Military Operations Directorate of Indian Army in 1947 and "now in 1971 Yahya is the President of Pakistan and I am the Chief of Indian Army."

He recalled that ***"in the pre-partition period he owned a red James motorcycle. Yahya, before moving to Pakistan persuaded Sam to sell it to him for Rs 1000. Sam agreed to it and Yahya drove-off on the motor bike promising to send the money from Pakistan but in the turmoil of partition he never paid the Rs 1000 to me but now he has paid me with half his country."***

Sam, gracious as always, went on to add that *"Yahya was a good man and a good soldier, we served together. He did not have a mean bone in his body."*

Post retirement, Field Marshal Sam Manekshaw served as the Chairman of a famous private sector organisation. For some financial irregularities the Company's Board of Directors was superseded by the Government and a retired civil servant Mr Naik was appointed its chairman. Sam on hearing of this appointment remarked that it is the first time in the history of armies in the world that *"a Field Marshal has been replaced by a Naik"* which in army parlance denotes a lower rank subordinate.

General K V Krishna Rao, Chief of the Army Staff in 1981 to 1983, in his foreword to a Biography of Sam has best described Sam Manekshaw's qualities of head and heart and leadership of Indian army in the following words:

> ***"India's greatest military leader during the worst crisis the country was forced into and how he emerged totally victorious, changing the course of history and elevating the nation to a significantly high level where it is taken into consideration as a country that matters much on international relations and is respected. It is not merely meant for the Armed Forces but also for political leaders and administrators and indeed the general public who are all responsible for the security and future of the Nation".***

I regard my tenure of two years' service on the Army Headquarters under Sam Manekshaw's dynamic leadership as a highlight my service career.

17

Bangkok Agreement 1975
Asia's First Regional Trade Agreement

In the post-cold war scenario, regional cooperation in trade emerged as one of the most important realities of the Asia-Pacific region.

India, along with four other Asian countries - Bangladesh, Republic of Korea, Laos and Sri Lanka took the initiative, under the aegis of the United Nations Economic and Social Commission (ECAFE) to negotiate the Asian region's first multi-member trade agreement leading to the establishment of the "First Agreement on Trade Negotiations Among the Developing member countries of UN-ESCAP" in 1975, also known as the Bangkok Agreement.

I represented the nodal Ministry of Commerce (Foreign Trade Division) and co-ordinated the representations of the inter-ministerial teams during the negotiations in the various meetings held between 1973-75.

Consensus was built among the 5 original negotiating countries after several rounds of meetings between their delegations consisting of the representatives of their respective Ministries of Commerce, External Affairs, Finance, Petroleum, Chemical, Shipping and Transport on exchange of tariff concession on items of trade concerning them.

The Bangkok Agreement's aim was to promote inter-regional trade through the exchange of mutually agreed tariff measures and move forward to liberalisation in investments, services, other trades facilitation in the region. Consequent to these negotiations, the Bangkok Agreement emerged as the first Preferential Trade Agreement (PTA) of the region and the only such agreement that links East and South Asia as well as the two most populous countries in the world, India and China which acceded to it in 2001.

The Bangkok Agreement, now renamed as Asia-Pacific Trade Agreement (APTA) aims to promote economic development of its member countries through the adoption of mutual beneficial trade liberalisation measures that contribute to regional trade expansion and economic co-operation.

It initially focused on tariff concessions on merchandise trade. It has now moved forward to negotiating trade liberalisation in Investment, Services, Trade Facilitation and working towards improving the economies of the member countries.

The two year long negotiations culminated in the consensus reached among the negotiating member countries in the penultimate round of negotiations.

The UN-ESCAP organised a formal signing ceremony attended by the diplomatic representatives of all member countries stationed in Bangkok on 31st July, 1975 at its headquarters in Sala Santitham, Bangkok.

The representatives of the five original negotiating countries: India, Bangladesh, Laos, Korea and Sri Lanka signed the historic Bangkok Agreement.

I had the privilege of representing India at the signing ceremony as the Chief Negotiator and Signatory to the Bangkok Agreement, along with the Ministers and Plenipotentiaries of the other four original negotiating countries on 31st July, 1975.

1975: Signing for India the Bangkok Agreement on Tariff Preferences L to R: H.E. Mr Maramis Executive Secretary UN - Escap, Mr R.K. Puri Leader, Indian Delegation and Mr Prok Amranand.

It was a moment of great honour for me to present the Instrument of Ratification of the Bangkok Agreement by the Government of India. Signed by The President Fakhruddin Ali Ahmed it read:

"I Fakhruddin Ali Ahmed, President of India,
do, hereby,
Ratify the First Agreement On Trade and Negotiations among the Developing Member Countries of UN -ESCAP
duly signed by India's authorised representative,
Rajendra Kumar Puri
on 31 July-1975 at Bangkok."

The significance of the agreement, the first of its kind, was highlighted by Mr Raul Uranga of UNCTAD at the signing ceremony as providing for a continuing process of negotiations between the member countries.

ESCAP's Executive Secretary, H.E. Mr J B P Maramis stated that "it has been a huge step forward for the participating countries of Asia to achieve this Agreement, considering the immensity of the region and the diversity of the cultures and the political and economic systems.

Mr Maramis added that "the eight countries which have agreed to be signatories of the Bangkok Agreement have a total population of over 850 billion people, a land area more than 2 million square miles, and a total international trade 30 billion US dollars".

Mr Prok Amranand, Chief of International Trade Division of ESCAP expressed the hope that this agreement may one day emerge as a significant step towards creation of an Asian Economic Community.

18

India Tea Centre, London 1977-79

In 1958, the High Commissioner of India to the United Kingdom, with her vision and drive, Mrs Vijay Lakshmi Pandit in consultation with her brother Prime Minister Jawahar Lal Nehru, decided on acquiring a grandiose three storeyed building located at the junction of Bond Street and Oxford Street, London's busiest shopping street credited with receiving a million footfalls daily.

The India Tea Centre came up on the entire ground floor, with seating for about 100 guests, serviced by Indian staff, mostly students, on a part time basis, under the supervision of trained and qualified Indian Lady demonstrators.

In 1977, I was appointed as the Director of Tea Promotion for UK, Ireland and Scandinavian Countries. The Directorate was declared an attached office of the Indian High Commission and received full support from the then High Commissioner Mr B K Nehru and the Deputy High Commissioner, Mr Natwar Singh.

With the change of Government in India, Mr N G Goray, a veteran political leader was appointed High Commissioner and Mr P A Nazareth, a career diplomat, as the Deputy High Commissioner. They extended their fullest support in all our promotional activities and attended all our functions:

High Commissioner
Mr N G Goray signing the visitors book.
The author and his wife Mrs Uma Puri are seen to the right.

With Mata Nirmala Devi and Mr C P Srivastava, Secretary General of the Inter-governmental Maritime Consultative Organisation.

Mr N G Goray attending a meeting of the British Tea Council at the Tea Centre, with Mr R K Puri delivering the welcome address.

The author with Mr E L Attridge, UK Secretary for Food (centre) and Mr P K Dave, India's Ambasador to the EEC (now EU)

L to R: Mr Guy Routledge, a leader of the British Tea Trade talking to Mr Prakash Tandon, Chairman STC, the author and Mr Deepak Roy from the Indian Tea trade.

L to R Mrs Isobel Nazareth, (wife of the Indian Deputy High Commissioner) the author and his wife, Mrs Uma Puri

With Ms Ann Morrow, journalist with The Daily Telegraph

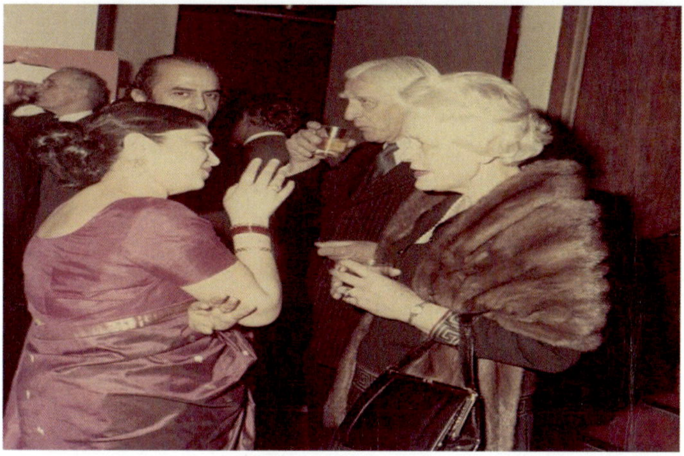

With Sir Peter and Lady Banyard (1980)

The author with Mrs. Attridge, Secretary, Ministry of Agriculture, U.K, Mr. Attridge and Mr. P.K. Kaul, Secretary, Commerce, India.

The High Commissioner of India, Mr N G Goray, a veteran Jan Sangh leader participated in all Tea Board events and vice versa my wife Mrs Uma Puri along with the Centre's team attended all High Commission events graced by eminent visitors like Her Royal Highness Princess Margaret and Her Royal Highness Princess Alexandra:

With HRH Princess Margaret (1977)

With HRH Princess Alexandria (1978)

India Tea Centre at Oxford Street was visited by the world's top Tea Trade Buyers like Lord Routledge, Sir John Jardine Patterson, Sir John Banyard, Mrs Attridge, British Secretary of Agriculture and other important dignitaries like the then Commerce Secretary, Mr P K Kaul,

I promptly called the lady and confirmed our acceptance of her gracious invitation.

On arrival at her splendid mansion, we were received by two turbaned Indian attendants and escorted to her spacious lounge where a few guests were already present.

The hostess, dressed in a sari, received us at the door where we introduced ourselves. I was the last one in and as I mentioned my name, she smiled and told me that her niece had conveyed my desire, to meet Gina Lollobrigida. With one sweeping gesture of her hand, she turned towards one side and said 'She is here! Let me take you to her.' I stood rooted, too amazed to move or say anything.

She introduced me and all other members of our delegation to the iconic actress. We all gathered around the film celebrity for a lively chat. She enlightened us about the biography of Imelda Marcos, wife of the then President of Philippines, Ferdinand Marcos. The book was titled "the Philippines" by Gina Lollobrigida.

I requested her for an autograph for my daughter, which she gave graciously on a blank card provided by our generous hostess. Gina Lollobrigida left soon afterwards, promising to not only visit India but also write a book on India.

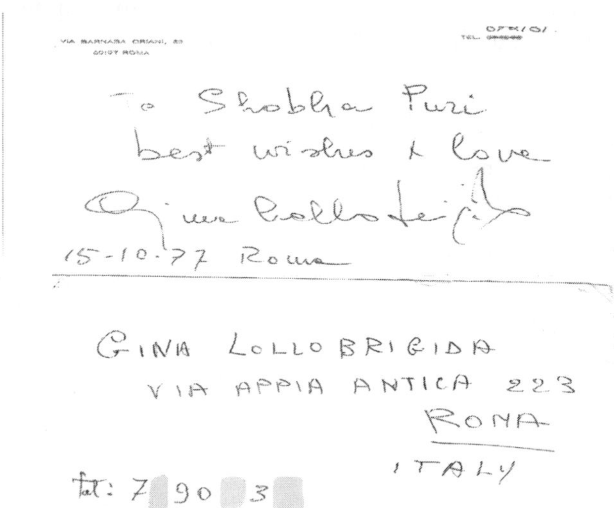
To Shobha Puri
best wishes & love
Gina Lollobrigida
15-10-77 Roma

GINA LOLLOBRIGIDA
VIA APPIA ANTICA 223
ROMA
ITALY
tel: 7 90 3

It was perhaps the most pleasant and memorable experience we all had.

NOTE: Names of the Indian hostess and her niece have not been mentioned for privacy reasons.

20

Hobson's Choice - Gina Lollobrigida or the Pope

In November 1979, I was invited to join an Indian Inter-Ministerial Delegation, headed by Mr P K Kaul, then Additional Secretary, Ministry of Commerce to Rome. It also included three or four senior representatives of the Indian Tea Trade.

The Senior Lady Tea Demonstrator at the India Tea Center was requested to confirm my hotel booking at Rome and convey my preference for vegetarian food to the hotel.

She advised me that vegetarian food at the hotel could be a problem and perhaps her aunt, an Indian princess, married to an Italian Count, could be of help. She added that, if desired, her aunt could also set up an audience with the Pope for the Indian Delegation!

I thanked her and remarked in a light vein that some of the delegates may perhaps prefer meeting 'Gina Lollobrigida' rather than the Pope.

In Rome, the members of Indian delegation, after having partaken of Italian cuisine for two or three days began to look for Indian restaurants.

The next day I received a call from an Indian lady, who introduced herself as the aunt of the lady Tea demonstrator of my office at London and invited us to have dinner at her family home. I thanked her for the invite and agreed to consult the leader of my delegation and revert back to her.

I met Mr Kaul in his suite where other members of the delegation were also present. We were also joined that evening by a former Indian Ambassador to Italy, (one Mr Haksar if memory holds after 5 decades).

The delegates were all pleased to be invited for a vegetarian meal at an Indian home, egged on by Mr Atal who seemed to know her and assured us of a pleasant get together at her mansion. He also asked to be included in the group for the proposed evening get together.

19

When Morarji Desai Laughed

An amusing incident occured during Prime Minister Morarji Desai's visit to London, accompanied by the then Foreign Minister Mr Atal Behari Vajpayee. The Indian High Commissioner Mr Goray convened a meeting of all Indian officials of the High Commission and its attached offices to be addressed by Mr Morarji Desai.

Morarji Desai being of a taciturn temperament, addressed the gathering for some twenty minutes, heard by the audience in rapt silence. It was a litany of the Janata Government's achievements under his leadership. The audience greeted it with a civil clapping of hands.

Morarji then announced that, if anyone, wishes to ask a question, he may do so. None asked. The silence was becoming embarrassing. Mr Goray intervened and enjoined the staff to ask any question they wished to ask the Prime Minister.

Sensing a lack of response, one staff member, a Sikh officer stood up and asked the Prime Minister if there is any proposal to stop levy of a pay cut of 3% each month towards Bangladesh Fund. He added that the Bangladesh war ended in 1971 but the cut is levied every month even now in 1978.

Morarji Desai appeared rather annoyed by the question and advised the questioner to raise this issue with the High Commissioner, and not with the Prime Minister.

The questioner resumed his seat. No further question was asked. The High Commissioner gracefully thanked the Prime Minister and the meeting was declared closed.

The High Commissioner then escorted the Prime Minister through the Hall's midway, acknowledging greetings of the staff standing on either side.

As they approached close to where the Sikh gentleman was standing, Morarji stiffened. Sensing trouble, Mr Goray whispered to the Prime

Minister that the Sikh gentleman was the victim of a knife attack by the Anand Margis in London.

Morarji immediately softened and halted near the questioner and asked him if the wound had healed.

Prompt came the reply: “Sir, this wound has healed but this other wound of 3 percent pay cut continues to hurt each month for the last 7 years, although Bangladesh was liberated in 1971.”

The Sardar’s robust response made Morarji Desai laugh. He turned to High Commissioner Mr Goray and advised him to convey his message to the Finance Minister to notify the cancellation of the 3 percent cut towards the Bangladesh fund with immediate effect from the salaries of all Indian employees of Indian diplomatic missions worldwide.

Prime Minister Morarji Desai and British Prime Minister James Callaghan bilateral meeting on mutual cooperation between the two countries received wide coverage in the media at home and in England.

On conclusion of the bilateral talks, Prime Minister Morarji Desai hosted a return banquet attended by British Prime Minister James Callaghan and his Cabinet colleagues was in a comic strip of a leading British newspaper the next day showing the two Prime Ministers raising a toast. It had James Callaghan looking somewhat suspiciously at the contents in his glass, a satire on Morarji’s preference for certain kinds of aperitifs.

(later Cabinet Secretary), Mr PK Dave, Ambassador to the EEC, Sir Peter Parker, Chairman of British Rail and others.

In 1977, Oxford Street came heavily under terror attacks mounted by the IRA attackers. On a single day in 1977 thirteen bombs detonated in and around Oxford Street, wrecking and setting shops on fire. Access to India Tea Centre became difficult. The situation got further compounded by the Morarji Desai Government in India banning the extremist Anand Marg Organisation and imprisoning its Guru, Prabhat Ranjan Sarkar, on a murder charge. This led to an outbreak of violent attacks against Indian Diplomats in Washington, London and other capitals by the followers of the sect.

The situation became alarming in Oxford Street establishments. The Deputy High Commissioner, Mr P A Nazareth intervened on behalf of the Tea Centre with the British Foreign and Home Offices to secure round the clock vigilance for the Centre from Scotland yard and other concerned security agencies of the British Government.

It was during this period that a newly arrived Indian employee of the High Commission was subjected to a knife attack which he however, survived due to prompt medical care.

21

A High Point of London Society

It is a time-honoured tradition of the British monarchy to host three Annual Garden Parties each summer at the Buckingham Palace.

Approximately, 8000 guests are invited for each party. In order to ensure that a cross-section of people attend, quotas are reserved for Diplomatic Corps. Civil Services, Armed Forces as well as Charities and Societies.

The Palace gates are opened from 3:00 p.m. for the guests to start arriving. The party officially begins when the Queen, accompanied by other members of the Royal family enters the garden at 4:00 p.m. and the National Anthem is played by one of the military bands.

The Queen and the late Duke of Edinburgh circulate among the guests through lanes. Each member of the Royal family takes a different route and random conversations are held with the guests lining up on either side of the lanes.

The Queen then reaches the Royal Tea tent where the high ranking Civil and Diplomatic Corps guests and the Foreign Dignitaries are assembled.

During my three-year tenure in London as the Director of Indian Tea Promotion in UK, Ireland and Scandinavia, I received an invitation from the Indian Lord Chamberlain of England inviting me, my wife and daughter to the Garden parties hosted by Her Majesty Queen Elizabeth.

EIIR

The Lord Chamberlain is
commanded by Her Majesty to invite
Shri Raj Kumar Puri and Shrimati Puri
and Kumari Shobha Puri
to a Garden Party at Buckingham Palace
on Tuesday, 10th July, 1979 from 4 to 6 p.m.

Morning Dress, Uniform or Lounge Suit

At the third garden party attended by me, my wife and daughter on 10th July 1979, we had the opportunity of meeting Lord Mountbatten.

He entered our lane and stopped by to exchange a word or two with guests at random. He had a brief chat with my daughter about her schooling in London, with my wife about her social activities and with me about my work for promotion of tea in UK and specially in Scandinavian countries.

Queen's Garden Party, Buckingham Palace (1978)
L to R: Mr & Mrs Sareen,
in the Centre: Mrs Uma Puri, Ms Shobha Puri and Mrs. Renu Kaul

22

Mountbatten's Missed Appointment

Lord Louis Mountbatten was the last British Viceroy of India who presided over the transfer of power from Britain to the Dominions of India and Pakistan on 15th August 1947.

Lord Louis Mountbatten was a gifted conversationalist. He could hold his own on almost any subject on earth.

I saw him arriving at the Royal Garden Party at the Buckingham Palace on 10th July 1979, accompanying Her Majesty Queen Elizabeth and other Royal family members.

As the military band finished playing the National Anthem of Britain, the Queen and other members of Royal family circulated among the various lanes lined on either side by the invited guests.

I noticed Lord Mountbatten entering the lane in which I was standing with my wife and daughter.

Lord Mountbatten was stopping to talk to guests of various nationalities and had something or the other to say to them.

He stopped by us, had a brief chat with my daughter about her schooling in London, with my wife about her social activities and with me about plans for promotion Indian Tea in UK, Ireland and Scandinavian countries.

Or learning about my office being located at the junction of Old Bond Street and Oxford Street and displaying a signboard saying India Tea Centre, he immediately recalled that his good friend, Mrs Vijaylaxmi Pandit, the Indian High Commissioner, had invited him to its opening function in the 50's but to his regret he was unable to attend it.

I immediately invited him to visit The India Tea Centre and fulfil his commitment to his good friend, Mrs Pandit. He promptly asked me what he would be required to do there.

I sensed an opportunity of generating high visibility for Indian teas in the media and the trade and mentioned to him that we have recently received very high quality Indian tea grown in the upper reaches of Darjeeling for launch in the United Kingdom, which he could do the honour of launching during his visit to the centre.

For greater effect I added that if he launches the new tea, we will call it the Mountbatten Caddy.

He was visibly pleased at the suggestion and turning to the Aide accompanying him, asked him to co-ordinate with me and set up a mutually convenient date and time for his visit to the India Tea Centre to launch the Mountbatten Caddy.

The Aide called me three days later to ask if a date in the middle of the first fortnight of September 1979 would be suitable for the launch of Mountbatten Caddy.

I informed the High Commissioner, Mr N.G. Goray who readily agreed to attend the launch function and receive Lord Mountbatten. I then confirmed the date to his Aide.

Destiny had, however, other plans for Lord Mountbatten. He was assassinated by a bomb planted on board the fishing boat in Mullaghmore County Sligo in Ireland on 27th August, 1979.

The opportunity of welcoming him at the India Tea Centre was lost. Instead, we shut down the Centre as a mark of our respect for him on the day of the funeral procession of his cortège to Westminster Abbey.

Mountbatten missed on the day.

23

Prince Charles' India Connection

I recall meeting Prince Charles at the Food and Beverage Exhibition at the Earl's Court Exhibition Centre, London, in 1978, though, four decades later, memory could be hazy about the year. Historically, the Earl's Court Exhibition Centre has been the chosen venue for teas of the world and Indian tea since it first arrived from Assam in 1837. Its fifty-year Jubilee, which coincided with Queen Victoria's Golden Jubilee in 1887, was celebrated at this Exhibition Centre with great pomp as an icon of British imperialism.

I was in London from 1977 to 1980 as the Tea Board of India's overseas Director of Tea Promotion for UK, Ireland and the Nordic countries: Denmark, Finland, Iceland, Norway, Sweden as well as Greenland and Faroe Islands.

The Tea Board had a very visible presence in London. It had acquired, shortly after India's independence, a large 3-Storeyed building, on London's busiest shopping street, the Oxford Street. The India Tea Centre was located on the ground floor (basement was utilised for conferences and get togethers) and the Director's office was located on its first floor.

Prince Charles inaugurated the F & B Exhibition that year at the Earl's Court Exhibition Centre. He visited the stall of each participating country, evincing keen interest in the Food and Beverage products on display. Ahead of the Prince, walked his security detail, discreetly cautioning the exhibitors not to offer food or beverage items to the Prince to taste.

I received the Prince at the Tea Board's stall at the exhibition and introduced him to our staff on duty at the Indian Teas stall. Among them were two professionally qualified Indian Lady Tea Demonstrators. They were handing out the much in demand steaming hot cups of Darjeeling, Nilgiri or Assam teas to the visitors at our stall.

Prince Charles engaged them in a lively conversation about the right way of brewing tea of which he seemed to have considerable expertise. Sniffing the aroma of the tea, then on the boil, the Prince enquired if it was cardamom.

The Lady Demonstrator promptly told him that the aroma was not of cardamom, but of a special Indian spice which, she added, perhaps His Royal Highness may not be familiar with. Prince Charles' curiosity aroused, he simply said: "Test me". The lady promptly poured the steaming tea in a dainty porcelain cup and, avoiding the disapproving look of the security detail, offered it to the Prince.

Charles raised the cup to his lips, sniffed the tea and put the cup down, on the counter saying "I know what the spice is". Saying that, he pulled out a small silver phial from his jacket pocket, opened its lid to display clove buds nestling in it. The Lady Demonstrator was flummoxed.

A while later she enquired from the Prince why he carries cloves with him. Charles then mentioned to her that in public life he has to give a speech or two at functions almost daily. That, at times, leaves his throat parched and rather strained.

An Indian friend had presented him the cloves, advising him to chew one or two cloves prior to making a speech. He found it helpful. Thus, began his Indian connection, said the Prince, with a laugh, and moved on to the next stall.

The bonhomie created by the Prince at our stall encouraged me to mention to him that a special caddy of the finest quality of tea grown in the Darjeeling hills has been received from the Tea Board headquarters in Calcutta (now known as Kolkata) for presentation to Her Majesty the Queen and requested for his help in arranging it.

The Prince remarked that his mother, the Queen, adores the flavour of Darjeeling tea and would be delighted to savour the high quality tea sent for her by the Indian Tea Board. He then directed his Aide to co-ordinate with the Equerry to the Queen to receive the caddy of Darjeeling tea on her behalf.

The Caddy of Tea was duly delivered at the Buckingham Palace and acknowledged by the Equerry in a letter to me which read:

"The Royal Equerry is commanded by Her Majesty the Queen to convey her sincere thanks to the Tea Board of India for the generous gift of Darjeeling tea. Her Majesty looks forward to savouring the high-grade Indian tea shortly".

I spoke to the Equerry, thanked him for his prompt acknowledgement and asked him "how short is short" ? The Equerry explained that any new food or beverage item received for Her Majesty's consumption has to undergo several lab trials prior to serving to her. **The trials, he added, could take a year or more!**

24

Palace-On-Wheels

Forty years ago, is a long time for today's generation to know of the race to roll out first; it took place between two of the most famous luxury tourist trains of the world, **'Palace-on-Wheels'** in India and the **'Venice - Simplon - Orient Express in Europe.**

As it transpired the Palace-on-Wheels was flagged off on its inaugural journey from Old Delhi's metre gauge platform amidst much fanfare on 26th January 1982.

The remodelled Venice – Simplon - Orient Express rolled out on its maiden journey from London's Victoria Station, serenaded by a band and passengers in period costume toasted with champagne on 25th May 1982.

I was closely associated with this historic competition between two of the most popular tourist trains: the Palace - on - Wheels in India and the Orient Express in Europe.

During my 3 years tenure as Director, Tea Board of India in London, my office though located on Oxford Street, was administratively attached to the High Commission of India located at Aldwych. The India Tea Centre on the ground floor (with the office of the Tea Board of India on the first floor), of a building located most centrally on the Oxford Street, was a popular landmark for shoppers and visitors to meet. It was the venue for holding demonstration of variety of Indian Teas and for organising tea promotions for media representatives and buyers of tea.

During this assignment in London, I met the Chairman of British Railway Board, Sir Peter Parker, a few times to explore the possibility of introducing Indian teas on the British rail system which was one of the largest consumers of tea in England.

I once met James Sherwood, President of the Sea Containers Group in Sir Peter Parker's office during one of my visits there. He was a rail enthusiast and had purchased a few of the carriages of the original

Orient Express which operated from Paris to Constantinople (Istanbul) from 1883 to 1977.

James Sherwood was getting the coaches restored and refurbished at a Rail Workshop in Calais for launching a luxury train to be called the "Venice-Simplon Orient Express" between London and Venice. He visited my office on Oxford Street a few times to discuss plans for launching an Oriental Eastern Orient Express between Singapore-Bangkok-Calcutta to know how the Indian Railways would support it.

On completion of my three-year tenure of posting in London, I returned to India in January 1980 and was appointed Director, Tourism and International Co-operation Division of Railway Board.

1980 was a seminal year for India. The Olympic Association had allotted the 9th Asian Games to be held in Delhi in December 1982. It was the second largest multi-sport event of the world after the Olympics, and was expected to be attended by 10,000 athletes, sports officials, dignitaries from about 40 countries.

The Government of India had appointed a high powered Organising Committee headed by a senior political figure with the mandate for complete image makeover of Delhi as a world class city with construction of requisite number of sports stadia, hotels, flyovers, widening of roads and other connected facilities. I represented Railway Board in the meetings of the Organising Committee.

At one of the meetings of the Organising Committee of Asian Games, attended by the then Chairman of the Railway Board, Mr MS Gujral and myself, it was proposed that Indian Railways should offer exclusive rail excursions by special trains to historic sites on fully packaged basis inclusive of travel, meals and sightseeing.

The Asian Games were scheduled in Delhi from 18th November 1982 to 4th December 1982. The time available for devising and delivering this exclusive rail excursion by a special train was less than two years.

Mr Gujral, an iconic Railway Officer, decided to utilise the royal saloons of the former princely rulers of feudal states of Rajputana (Rajasthan) to be deployed for the proposed Asian Games Special Train which would offer options of tours to Jaipur-Udaipur-Jodhpur-Jaisalmer- Bharatpur- Agra and Delhi with options of 2 nights 3 day tours and 7 nights 8 days tours. The train would have facilities of sleeping cabins, attached WC, Dining Cars, Lounge, Staff Cars etc.

The proposal was discussed at the next meeting of the Games Organising Committee and unanimously approved. This led to the creation of India's most famous luxury tourist train aptly named as the Palace-on-Wheels.

The royal saloons of the former Maharajas of the princely states of Rajputana (Rajasthan) and Gujarat had been acquired by the Indian Railways after Independence and were no longer in use. These were assembled in the Locomotive Workshop at Ajmer for restoration and refurbishing in a very tight time schedule.

The fully fitted and restored 18 carriage train, consisting of 12 luxurious saloons, Dining Car, Lounge-cum-Bar carriage with a separate play area for children and a library, 2 Staff Cars and 2 Baggage cars, to be hauled by a highly polished and decorated steam engine proudly displaying its name, "Desert Queen" was ready in one year's time for trials which were run by the middle of 1981.

The trials were held on two itineraries of 2-nights 3-days called Take 1, another with 7-nights 8-day tour called Take 2. The shorter itinerary included visits to Jaipur and Udaipur and the longer itinerary covered Jaipur-Chittor-Udaipur-Jodhpur-Jaisalmer-Bharatpur-Agra. Both tours commenced from and terminated at Delhi Sarai Rohilla.

Regarding services on the tourist train, including housekeeping, valets in sleeping cars, cooking and serving of meals in Dining Cars and also the sightseeing tours at the tourist destinations, it was decided to make the Rajasthan Tourism Development Corporation a partner on revenue sharing basis.

Mr M S Gujral and I had a meeting with Rajasthan's then Chief Minister, late Mr Shiv Charan Mathur, during his visit to Delhi. Mr Mathur met us at Bikaner House, the State's Guest House in Delhi along with his team of tourism officials headed by the able and enthusiastic Managing Director of the Rajasthan Tourism Development Corporation, Mr Anand Prasad. They instantly agreed to be joint partners in the project with Indian Railways.

It was also decided to depute a team comprising Mr A V Poulose, Financial Commissioner Railways, I and Sudhir Verma, Secretary, Tourism of Rajasthan to London for a marketing meeting with leading British travel agents and tour operators. We were also required to study the facilities being planned on the Venice-Simplon-Orient Express at London during its trial phase.

Our meeting with the British tour operators and media representatives was held at the Westbury Hotel, Bond Street. The late Maharaja of Jaipur,

Bhawani Singh, a war hero and polo player, also attended the meeting which imparted an authentic royal touch to the interactions with media and travel representatives about the royal train – Palace-on-Wheels.

The meeting was a run-away success, making it to the front pages of British newspapers next day and the inaugural trip of Palace-on-Wheels scheduled on 26th January 1982 was a complete sell out.

We also held a meeting with James Sherwood at his imposing office at the Sea Container House on the South Bank of the River Thames in London. He called in his senior officials who acquainted us with the facilities planned in the Venice-Simplon Orient Express. They arranged our visit to the Orient Express parked in a railway yard at a London station.

On our return to India, a meeting of travel trade representatives was held at the Rail Bhawan to apprise them of the proposed launch of Palace-on-Wheels on 26th January 1982 as a joint project of the Indian Railways and Rajasthan Tourism Development Corporation. Preceding the formal launch, a few trial runs of the Palace-on-Wheels trains were organised and Trade and Media representatives were invited to travel and experience this unique offering by the Railways and Rajasthan Government.

MISSED DATE WITH JAMES BOND

An interesting episode that took place at Udaipur railway station when the Palace-on-Wheels was on its trial run. I received an urgent phone call from the Station Master Udaipur Railway Station to inform me that a Hollywood film unit was in Udaipur for the shooting of the movie **'Octopussy'**. The unit had booked a few coaches of a local train for a scene to be filmed with its star cast of Roger Moore and heroine Maud Adams on board.

The star cast saw the gleaming new train and desired to shift the shooting of a romantic scene between Roger Moore and Maud Adams on the Palace-on-Wheels.

Shooting scenes on a train in India are subject to compliance of certain mandatory provisions. The film unit was scheduled to fly out of India the next morning and consequently could not get the clearance in the short span of few hours they had at their disposal.

The Palace-on-Wheels missed an opportunity of getting global publicity in the **'Octopussy'** which still commands attention. It would have done for tourism in India what **"Crocodile Dundee"** did for Australian tourism.

The Palace-on-Wheels had its launch ceremony on 26th January 1982 attended by a distinguished gathering of dignitaries and tourism enthusiasts from the metre gauge platform of Delhi Main Railway station flagged off jointly by Union Railway Minister Mr P C Sethi, Rajasthan Chief Minister Mr S C Mathur and Union Tourism Minister Mr A P Sharma.

The Palace-on-Wheels has been a boon for tourism in India. It has motivated large number of tourists to visit India for rail excursions, spawned growth of hotels and created employment. It remains the flagship of Indian Tourism.

ORIENT EXPRESS RESTAURANT

In late 1981, Railway Board had a surprise visitor, James Sherwood. He was flying to Sydney and took a short stop over at Delhi. I arranged his meeting with Mr Gujral, Chairman, Railway Board. It was a warm and convivial meeting between the two. I also accompanied Mr Sherwood to the Palace-on-Wheels train at the Delhi Sarai Rohilla station. A lasting imprint of his visit to India is the Orient Express Restaurant at the Taj Palace Hotel, New Delhi, themed around his legendary train.

The Meter Gauge railway track in Rajasthan has been converted to Broad Gauge. Consequently, the original saloons of the Palace-on-Wheels have been replaced with a new wide bodied Broad Gauge Palace-on-Wheels which continues to offer a fabulous voyage of discovery to tourists and ranks among the five best luxury tourist trains of the world.

25

India Tourism Development Corporation : 1982 – 86

I was appointed Senior Vice President - Commercial of the India Tourism Development Corporation (ITDC) from 1983 to 1986.

Among the new schemes established by me were the ITDC's first worldwide reservation network through the Golden Tulip chain of KLM Royal Airlines, introducing socially motivated tourism packages for senior citizens and youth tourism in the ITDC chain of hotels and revamping the Duty Free Shops at all international airports in the country into major profit centres for the country.

On 31st October 1984, the country was stunned by the assassination of Prime Minister, Mrs Indira Gandhi by three of her bodyguards, in the aftermath of Operation Blue Star.

As news began to pour in of the arrival of world leaders to attend the funeral of Mrs Gandhi scheduled on 3rd November 1984, the ITDC had to swing into immediate action to get its flagship hotel, The Ashok, ready for accommodating the dignitaries and their security staff.

I had the responsibility of getting the Ashok Hotel vacated by relocating the guests staying there to other hotels of the city to enable security teams to check, sanitise and secure the hotel's premises.

Among the world leaders arriving in Delhi to attend Mrs Gandhi's funeral were the British Prime Minister Margaret Thatcher, Queen Elizabeth's daughter Princess Anne, Pakistan President Zia-ul-Haq, Australian Prime Minister Bob Hawke, Zimbabwe Robert Mugabe, Y. Nakasone, Japanese Prime Minister and numerous other leaders.

The 550 room Ashok Hotel was almost fully vacated by the evening of 1st November, 1984 barring one room which was occupied by a visiting Air Chief of a North American country.

The Embassy of that country made a special request to allow its Air Chief to stay on for one night only to enable him to attend a reception at the Embassy that evening with the assurance of vacating the room next morning. The security team agreed to make one exception for the Air Chief of a country.

The Air Chief and his wife returned after midnight and retired to their room.

On reaching their room, the Air Chief entered the bathroom to change and the wife went to the window to part the curtains when she gave a loud scream. The Air Chief came rushing out to see an armed man swinging from a tree towards their room.

The couple ran out of the room to the Reception area. The staff had a hard time calming them by explaining that the commandos of the security team were practicing entry into the room to rescue the occupants just in case a hostage situation arose.

The Air Chief and his wife refused to stay a moment longer at the hotel and contacted their Embassy which immediately sent a vehicle to take them to the Ambassador's residence for staying the night prior to flying back to their country the next morning.

Food Festival India

The next important event of ITDC, I recall is of leading a team of 80 officials, cooks and their assistants to Washington to organise a Food Festival of India to be held on the Mall from 28th June 1985 to 10th July 1985, which features in the following chapter.

26

Festival of India in Washington

During Prime Minister Indira Gandhi's official visit to USA in 1983, an INDO - US Cultural Agreement was signed by her and President Reagan.

In terms of the agreement, it was decided that India would participate in the Annual Smithsonian Folk Life Festival on the Washington Mall with a Festival of India, while over 1500 priceless artifacts would be on display at the National Gallery of Art.

Synchronising with the official visit of Prime Minister Rajiv Gandhi, in June 1985, the India Tourism Development Corporation (ITDC) was assigned the task of organising a Food Festival of India on the Washington Mall.

I was then Senior Vice President, ITDC and was privileged to lead a team of 80 Catering Managers, Chefs and Cooks of various hotels of ITDC. The team included Mr Anil Bhandari, then Vice President (Catering) and former General Manager of Ashok Hotel, Delhi, whose expertise as a hotelier was vital for the success of the Food Festival of India.

The Indian Embassy at Washington, led by Mr Peter Sinai as the then officiating Head of the Mission extended its full support in the planning and organising of the Indian Food Festival on the Washington Mall.

It enabled the ITDC team to put up 75 Food Stalls with cuisine from over 12 States. The pavilion for the Indian Food stalls was in an exclusive section of the Smithsonian Festival which offered easy access to visitors.

The formal opening of the Festival of India at the Kennedy Centre on 13th June, 1985, was done by Prime Minister Rajiv Gandhi and Mrs Nancy Reagan.

On 26th June, Washington woke up to see and hear unusual sights and sounds.... colourful festoons, vibrant dancers in colourful dresses swaying to bubbly music, display of Indian art and craft, (artisans giving live demonstrations), bangle sellers, puppeteers, acrobats etc., As the day progressed, the wafting aroma of Indian spices drew the crowds to the Washington Mall. The freshly prepared Indian delicacies,to tickle the taste buds, Indian bread baked in 'tandoors' (clay ovens had been flown in) fascinated the visitors!. Rope 'charpoys' were strewn across, to relax or get sun tanned. All parts of the village 'Mela' (fair) were recreated on the Mall. From day one, the Indian food stalls were a great hit, with streams of visitors queuing up to enjoy the delicacies.

As Washington's popular "Hop On, Hop Off" Bus Tours would halt near the Festival area in the afternoon, the bus driver would announce "If you are looking for a lunch stall, the best place to go to are the Indian Food Stalls". This generated huge crowds of visitors, who enjoyed the 75 food stalls at the fair, danced to Indian music, admired the handicrafts and the skill of the craftsmen.

We also had a large number of Indian residents of America (NRIs) driving in from various cities visiting the Festival of India and revelling in the festive atmosphere.

GOOD MORNING, AMERICA

I recall visiting some of the other pavilions of the Smithsonian Folk Life Festival. At one of them I noticed a Mobile TV van covering live scenes of the pavilions at the Smithsonian Folk Life festival for news broadcast.

During our interaction I invited them to the Indian Pavilion and be our guests at the Indian Food Festival. This idea appealed to them and they agreed to come to Indian Pavilion to do a 'live' TV clip for their "Good Morning America" show broadcast next day.

I had an exclusive table laid out for the live show with a sampling of the Indian savouries (Samosas) and sweets (Jalebi), not to forget the spicey Tandoori Chicken and Naans (Indian breads) hot off the clay ovens!. The team's OB Van (Outdoor Broadcast Van) drove up to the Indian pavilion for the coverage. My senior catering Managers and waiters dressed in traditional Indian attire and turbans acquainted them with the delicacies.

The live broadcast by the team as they relished the Indian spread, assured hoards of visitors!

The team leader of the OB van team invited me to give an interview during the broadcast. Handing over the mike and requested me to respond to the questions he would put to me as soon as he got the signal.

It was an interesting experience appearing on the 'Good Morning America'. The interview featured 'breaking news' reporting on the Food Festival of India, covering live the Indian delicacies being made and the question-answer session with me and concluding with the remark that "If you are on the Mall, the place you must go to is the Indian Food Festival".

The TV team thanked me for the hospitality extended to them and presented a cassette of the recording as a memento.

SENATOR MOYNIHAN

Among the American dignitaries who visited the Festival of India were Senator Moynihan, former American Ambassador to India and his daughter Maura Moynihan, a very popular social activist friend of India.

The Senator and his daughter spent some time going around the various stalls and spoke briefly about his great admiration for India. We were then joined by a young diplomat of the Indian Embassy who was visiting the festival with his family.

I recall the young diplomat asking the senator "Who in your opinion is more important, Ambassador or Senator, since you have been in both positions".

The Senator smiled and replied: "Ambassador, as he can snooze in the afternoon, a Senator cannot". The young diplomat had no further question to ask.

Senator Moynihan, Former US Ambassadar to India with Mr R.K. Puri (centre)
at the Indian Food Festival Organised at the Washington Mall in July 1985
Ms Moynihan looks on

27

Asian Panorama

In 1996, "ASIAN PANORAMA", a Tourism Magazine, did a cover story on my significant contributions to tourism as the Creator of Palace-on-Wheels on the eve of my retirement.

ASIAN PANORAMA

THE CREATOR OF PALACE-ON-WHEELS

"Appointed to the Indian Railway Traffic Service in 1962, Mr R. K. Puri is currently Adviser, Ministry of Railways in the rank of Additional secretary to the Government of India.

During his long and distinguished career, he has held important assignments in several ministries, public sector undertakings and autonomous bodies of the Government of India at national and international levels. He was Director, Rail Movements, Ministry of Defence during the War of 1971, Director (foreign trade) Ministry of Commerce and was deputed by the Government of India to London for three years as Director tea promotion, UK and Scandinavia, (1977 -80). He has also worked as Consultant to the United Nations.

He had a continuous and varied innings in tourism since 1980 when he was appointed to head the newly set up tourism and international co-operation division of the ministry of railways. He innovated the world famous Palace-on-Wheels luxury tourist train in 1981 which has become a major foreign exchange earner for the country. He planned and introduced the Great Indian tourist train in Buddhist sector in 1982 and was responsible for establishing the GSA network of Indian Railway now functioning in over 15 countries.

The ministry of tourism utilised his expertise in tourism in 1983 as Senior Vice President, India Tourism Development Corporation. He established ITDC's first worldwide reservation network through the Golden Tulip chain of KLM Royal Airlines, introduced socially motivated tourism pack ages for Senior Citizens and youth tourism in the ITDC chain of hotels and revamped the Duty Free Shops at all international airports in the country into a major profit centre for the Corporation".

In 1986, the planning commission appointed him as Secretary of the high powered National Committee on Tourism, in which capacity, he contributed to the evolving of the new national tourism policy which has led to the liberalisation of the tourism sector.

In 1987, he was appointed the founder Director of the Indian Institute of Tourism and Travel Management, the apex organisation of the Ministry of Tourism for tourism education in India. During his tenure, the institute emerged as a national centre of tourism education. Its regional chapters were established and linkages were forged with leading universities in India and abroad.

In 1990, he authored a comprehensive compendium of Tourism Curricula comprising of management development programmes, training of trainer programmes and the post graduate degree course of master of tourism administration (MTA). It has since then been adopted by several universities in India and in South Asia.

He was chief Negotiator and Signatory for India in the Bangkok Agreement on tariff preferences among developing countries of ESCAP. He gained extensive experience of bilateral and multilateral co-operation among countries of the United Nations-ESCAP and World Trade Organisations.

ESCAP also utilised his services as a regional expert for the establishment of the Asia Pacific Railway Corporation Group (APRCG) at Bangkok. He formulated on behalf of ESCAP the regional strategies for development of rail tourism which were adopted at the meeting of ministers of tourism of ESCAP countries in Tokyo.

As Adviser to the Ministry of Railways since 1992, he has introduced and implemented the concept of private sector participation in the development of rail transport infrastructure and services. This has been achieved by the innovative packaging of five tourist trains through the private sector on ownership and management basis. It has motivated world famous tourist train companies like Orient Express, Royal Scotsman and Wagon Lits to offer marketing and management franchise. He has pioneered the concept of fully packaged rail weekend holidays on Indian Railways which have been launched to 38 tourist destinations and has formulated a mega project for setting up one hundred budget hotels at railway stations in joint venture arrangements with private sector.

In the echelons of tourism administrators and planners in India, Mr R K Puri is among the most experienced. A tourism innovator par excellence, he is best known as the creator of Palace-on-Wheels in the 80's which has emerged as the flag ship of modern Indian tourism and as the author of the country's first Post Graduate Degree course in Tourism - the MTA which has laid the foundations of human resource development of tourism sector in India. His most recent creations, the 5 luxury tourist trains in the private sector and the proposed mega infrastructure project of 100 railway hotels being planned in the joint sector are a testimony of his commitment to tourism and will give a major thrust to enhancing India's tourism image.

His contributions to the human resource development of tourism sector received international recognition. He became the first recipient of PATA gold award for individual achievement in enhancement of tourism education, which was presented to him at the annual session at Vancouver in 1990. He was nominated as a member of PATA education authority, San Francisco for two consecutive terms in 1988 and 1991 and of the Education Council of World Tourism Organisation, Madrid in 1990. The World Tourism Organisation invited him to chair the Round Table on tourism education at Buenos Aires in 1991.

Widely travelled, he has led and been a member of Indian delegations to over 30 international conferences of United Nations - ESCAP, UNCTAD, UNIDO, GATT, ITC, ITPO, UIC, TREAME, WTO and PATA.

28

Field Marshal Manekshaw – Manekshawism

Sam Manekshaw was endowed with an extraordinary gift of spontaneous wit and humour which endeared him to all and enabled him to relate to people of all ages. His witty repartees or 'Manekshawism', a term that he had coined himself are presented in this chapter.

My assignment in the Army Headquarters offered me opportunities of observing during meetings Manekshaw's visionary style of leadership, grace, humility and humour. I also gleaned numerous anecdotes about him from published materials and those doing the rounds in army circles. The anecdotes admirably portrayed his character and personality.

In 1942, Sam as a young Captain participated in the Second World War in Burma. He led a successful bayonet charge against the Japanese in the Battle of Sitang River and was severely wounded, hit by 9 bullets in the stomach. His General-Officer-Commanding, Major General DT Cowan who witnessed the action recommended him for the award of Military Cross (MC) for exceptional bravery and had him evacuated to the field medical camp for emergency surgery. An apocryphal story recounts that the Surgeon, looked at his wound and enquired what happened to him. Sam replied ***"a bloody mule kicked me"***. The Surgeon gave a hearty laugh and said ***"by jove, you have some sense of humour and deserve to live"***. He operated upon Sam as best as he could. Sam survived and lived to wear the coveted Military Cross.

In the period preceding the Indo-Pak war, rumours were rife that the Indian army may seize power, just as the Pak army had done in the neighbouring country. An American diplomat who visited India around that time called on the Army Chief Sam Manekshaw along with the US Ambassador Kenneth Keating. In the course of conversation, he casually asked Sam when he was going to take over Sam's riposte ***"As soon as***

General Westmoreland takes over in your country" gave Ambassador Keating a hearty laugh.

In 1946, Sam Manekshaw and Yahya Khan in the rank of Lieutenant Colonel and Major respectively, became the first two Indian Army Officers to be posted to The Military Operations Directorate of the Army Headquarters, the preserve of English Officers till then. By coincidence during the Indo-Pak war of 1971 Field Marshal Manekshaw was the Chief of Indian Army and Field Marshal Yahya Khan was the President of Pakistan. After the war at a celebratory function in Delhi, Manekshaw related an amusing anecdote that ***"In 1946 before leaving for Pakistan, Yahya Khan persuaded me to sell my red motor cycle to him for a thousand rupees I agreed and Yahya took away the motorbike promising to send the money after reaching Pakistan. He never sent the money and now he has paid me with half his country".***

Manekshaw or Manekji?

Strange as it may sound, Sam Manekshaw, then a Lt. Colonel, was called 'Manekji' by Lord Mountbatten, the Viceroy of India. This became known to Prime Minister Nehru, Sardar Patel, and other leaders during a meeting (in October 1947), to decide on asking the Indian Army troops to Srinagar to prevent the town being captured by tribal fighters. The Viceroy asked Colonel Manekshaw:

"Manekji, please brief the Prime Minister and members of the Defence Committee on the ground situation prevailing in Srinagar"

Post retirement, many years later, in a recorded conversation with his grandson, Sam recounted this episode and added with a twinkle in his eye that Mountbatten used to call me, Manekji!

After the war, Sam was invited to Lahore for the delimitation talks. While there, he was invited to an officer's mess where he asked General Tikka Khan why he always wore dark glasses and added ***"You don't smoke, you don't drink and neither do you like pretty faces, I do all these things and still I don't hide my face".***

While inaugurating a new wing of the Defence Services Institute, Mhow, Manekshaw noticed that the new wing had not been properly furnished and pointed it out. He was promptly requested for additional funds Sam agreed to a generous grant from the Chief's Welfare Fund and then remarked ***"I just don't know how to say no. Sometimes I thank God for making me a man and not a woman. Can you imagine my condition if it had been otherwise. I would have been always pregnant".***

The Field Marshal's sense of humour was legendary while delivering the first Field Marshal Carriappa Memorial lecture in New Delhi in 1995 he said a lot has changed in the 60 years since he joined the army including the English language. When in his days someone said that ***"Capt. Manekshaw was Gay, he meant that he laughed and joked a lot. If an officer was being 'Queer' it meant, he would rather read Milton than join his friends for a hunt and General Officers were the only ones who had 'Aides'".***

He had a rather dim view of politicians and once remarked that ***"I wonder whether those of our political masters who have been put in-charge of the defence of our country can distinguish a mortar from a motor, a gun from a howitzer, a guerrilla from a gorilla, although a great many resemble the latter".***

His larger than life image as a victorious Army Chief caused nervousness in political circles and politicians were looking for a chance to cut him to size. Sam's penchant for witty remarks landed him in trouble with the powers that be. It transpired that Sam on landing at an airport was asked by a lady reporter "**if it were true, that Jinnah had offered him a high rank in the Pak Army and if so, why did he not accept it?"** Sam's off the cuff reply that, "Had I accepted Jinnah's offer and led the Pak army in war would India have won the war?" raised a storm in the Parliament, Sam became persona-non-grata with the Government, questions were asked in the House about the propriety of Sam's remark. Prime Minister Indira Gandhi chose to remain silent.

The Government withdrew his facilities of a Field Marshal including office, ADCs, bungalow, car etc. and his pay was reduced to a nominal pension although a Field Marshal is created for life and draws full pay till he lives.

Sam left Delhi on 15th July, 1973 with his wife and returned to Conoor. He was offered some diplomatic and gubernatorial appointments which he declined. He, however, accepted a few Directorships and Chairmanships of leading Companies.

He was a Director on the Board of Escorts when Lord Swaraj Paul, a London based businessman, made a bid to take over Escorts with the support of a few well placed politicians. The Government decided to reconstitute the entire Board with new nominees by ousting the existing Directors including Sam and appointed a retired bureaucrat, Mr Naik, as the Chairman. On knowing this, Sam with his inimitable wit remarked that ***"this is the first time a "Naik" has replaced a Field Marshal"***. Naik being a rank equivalent to a Corporal in the Indian Army.

In the twilight years of his life, at the age of 94, his health deteriorated and he was admitted to the Military Hospital in Wellington, Tamil Nadu. President Dr Abdul Kalam visited him there to enquire about his welfare. After meeting Sam, the President inscribed in the visitors book: ***"Doctors please take good care of the Field Marshal. The country owes a debt of gratitude to him".***

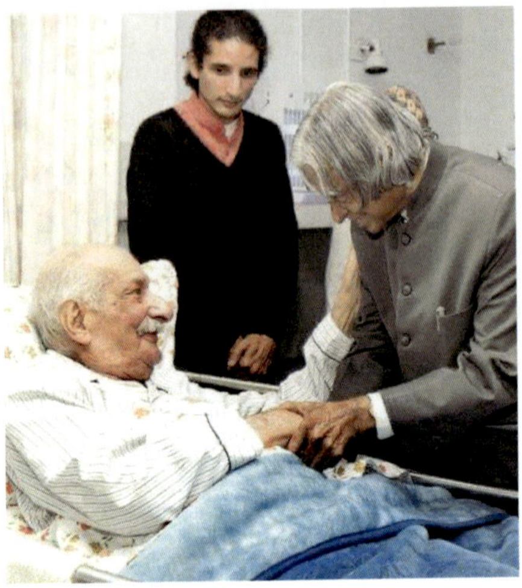

President of India, Dr Abdul Kalam with
Field Marshal Manekshaw

Touched by the sentiments inscribed by Dr APJ Abdul Kalam in the visitor's book, the doctors brought to his notice that Sam Manekshaw had been denied by the Government, his salary as a Field Marshal. On the intervention by Dr APJ Abdul Kalam, the then Prime Minister, Dr Manmohan Singh, ensured that not only would Sam Manekshaw receive his full arrears of pay and allowances but that the cheque be personally delivered at Wellington, by the then Secretary of Defence, Mr Shekhar Dutt. On receiving the cheque in his hospital bed, Sam smiled and in a feeble voice asked ***"Are you sure, it will not bounce"?***

Sam Manekshaw's qualities of head and heart have been best described by former Army Chief, General (retd.) K.V. Krishna Rao, later Governor of Jammu and Kashmir in his foreword to Major General (retd.) Shubi Sood's excellent book on ***"Leadership – Field Marshal Sam Manekshaw".***

"India's greatest military leader during the worst crisis that the country was forced into and how he emerged totally victorious, changing the course of history and elevating the Nation to a significantly high level

where it is taken into consideration as a country that matters much on International relations and is respected. It is not merely meant for the Armed Forces but also for political leaders, administrators and indeed the general public, who are all responsible for the security and future of the nation".

The lessons that emerge from the life of Field Marshal Sam Manekshaw are those of his visionary qualities of leadership, integrity, decision-making and concern for future leaders and citizens of India.

29

National Committee of Tourism: 1986-87

Rajiv Gandhi became the youngest Prime Minister at the age of 40 years on 24th October 1984, after the assassination of his mother, Mrs Indira Gandhi. He also held the post of the Minister of Tourism.

He had the vision of a young Prime Minister for the growth of tourism as contributor to the national GDP, creation of employment and facilitator of friendly relations with tourism generating countries.

Moving away from the earlier national policy of having a Five Year Plan for the growth of tourism in India, he directed the Planning Commission to set up a high powered National Committee on Tourism to prepare a long term perspective for the growth of tourism in India.

The Planning Commission of India, on a mandate from the Prime Minister, Mr Rajiv Gandhi, issued a notification on 10th June 1986, setting up a high powered National Committee on Tourism, headed by Mr Mohammed Yunus, Chairman of the Trade Fair Authority of India in the rank of a Cabinet Minister. It consisted of eleven members and a Secretary:

NATIONAL COMMITTEE ON TOURISM

June 1986 – November 1987

1. Chairman : Mr Mohammed Yunus
   Chairman
   Trade Fair Authority of India

Members:

2. Mr S K Misra, Secretary,
   Ministry of Tourism
3. Dr (Mrs) Kapila Vatsayanan,
   Secretary, Department of Arts

4. Mr K L Thapar,
   Advisor (Transport & Tourism), Planning Commission
5. Dr K B Lall ICS (Retd.),
   Former Commerce Secretary and Ambassador to EEC
6. Dr B Venkataraman
   Former Secretary, Ministry of Tourism
7. Mr A N Haskar
   Former Chairman, ITC
8. Mr Inder Sharma
   Chairman, SITA World Travel
9. Mr Gautam Khanna
   Senior Vice President, Oberoi Hotels and Chairman, Mercury Hotels
10. Mr A B Kerkar
    Vice Chairman & Managing Director, Taj Group of Hotels
11. Mr Rajan Jetley
    Managing Director, ITDC

Secretary

12. Mr R K Puri
    Senior Vice President, ITDC

The National Committee was mandated to:

(iv) Evaluate the economic and social relevance of international and national tourism of India.

(v) Define the tourism product in present and future variation, keeping in view market needs and demands.

(vi) Determine the requirements of balanced and integrated infrastructure and facilitation measures to achieve the maximum consumer satisfaction.

(vii) Develop a planned market strategy based on scientific research and consistent with ongoing responses of the market through a realistic communication strategy.

(viii) Determine and define the role of the Central Ministries, State Governments, Public and Private Sector Institutions in the promotion of tourism and suggest a mechanism for monitoring the performance of these agencies against a well-defined yardstick.

(ix) Assess the manpower needs for developing tourism sector and recommend appropriate training programmes for manpower development.

(x) Recommend organisational and institutional measures to systematise long term planning for the tourism sector on a sound technical, and economic basis.

The report of the National Committee on Tourism was one of the major achievements of 1987 in the arena of national tourism in India.

It was a major document and the first attempt to establish a master plan for accelerated development of tourism in India.

The recommendations made in the National Committee's report were arrived at in close consultation with the private sector travel industry and taking note of its perspective for future growth of tourism in India.

The Committee made strong recommendations to ensure that the ecological aspects of tourists are kept in view, be it the development of historical sites or in coastal or marine areas, mountain areas or wildlife sanctuaries to ensure that the carrying capacity of each area and infrastructural facilities are integrated into the development plans.

The National Committee on Tourism's recommendations focused on diversification of tourism in India from the traditional sightseeing tours of places of cultural interest to holiday tourism within the framework of the country's milieu with attention to aesthetic environmental and socio-cultural implications of tourism projects.

The National Committee on Tourism completed its assigned task in November 1987 and submitted its Report to Mr Rajiv Gandhi, Prime Minister of India in May 1988 at the Prime Minister's House.

National Committee On Tourism

The National Committee on Tourism, under the chairmanship of Mohamad Yunus, presented its Report to the Prime Minister in May 1988. The recommendations in it were prepared following close interaction with every segment of the travel industry.

Mr Mohd. Yunus presenting the report to Shri Rajiv Gandhi

The Chairman of the National Committee on Tourism, Mr Mohammed Yunus conveyed his commendation of my role as the Secretary of the Committee to Mr Abid Hussain, Member, Planning Commission as reproduced below:

Magna Carta of Tourism

D.O.No.CH:NCT:88

Mohammad Yunus
CHAIRMAN

National Committee on Tourism
Government of India
Pragati Bhawan Pragati Maidan
New Delhi 110001 INDIA

August 26, 1988

My dear Abid,

Now that we have completed the work of the National Committee on Tourism, I take this opportunity to place on record our deep appreciation of the work done by Shri R.K.Puri as Secretary of the Committee throughout its term of office - July'86 to June'88. He helped to guide the deliberations of the Committee by precise and well-researched documentation. He contributed in a large measure to the organising of sectoral studies and other inputs which facilitated the Committee's task of formulating a long term perspective plan of tourism development in the country.

I and my colleagues on the Committee shall be most happy if the outstanding work done by Shri Puri is placed on record in his CR Dossier. This is perhaps the least that we can do to accord recognition of a task well done.

With best wishes,

Yours sincerely,

(Mohammad Yunus)

Shri Abid Hussain,
Member,
Planning Commission,
Yojna Bhawan,
New Delhi.

The report of the National Committee on Tourism is a virtual Magna Carta with Ninety-Nine recommendations constituting ten chapters for the development of tourism in India.

Barring a few recommendations which have been implemented, the remaining have yet to see the light of day.

These include:

(vi) Creation of an independent National Tourism Board on par with the Railway Board of India in lieu of a Ministry of Tourism.

(vii) Creation of an All India Tourism Service consisting of tourism professionals recruited through the Union Public Service Commission on par with the other civil services.

(viii) Launching of Great Indian Rover train for the Buddhist sector on the pattern of Palace-on-Wheels Tourist train. It was created but not utilised for tourism purposes.

(ix) Nationalisation of vacant land at Railway Stations and Transport Depot in State for establishment of Hotels, Guest Lodges.

(x) State Governments to provide land as their equity for partnership with private sector entrepreneurs for establishment of hotels, motels, guest lodges in all villages, towns etc.

(xi) Proposal for setting up tourist hotels on Railway land at each train station.

These are among the several other recommendations of the National Committee of Tourism which deserve implementation.

BEACON OF LIGHT

Three and a half decades later, on July 16, 2021, Prime Minister Mr Narendra Modi while inaugurating India's first redeveloped Railway Station at Gandhi Nagar, Gujarat, has shown the beacon of light by calling for:

"The assets of Indian Railways can be utilised to turn into Centres for economic activity"

It raises the hopes for developing the recommendations of National Committee on Tourism as the new centres of national economic activity.

Mr Mohammad Yunus:

Chairman National Committee of Tourism (NCT)

No narrative of the National Committee on Tourism's report would be complete without a special mention of the role and contribution of its iconic Chairman, Mr Mohammed Yunus.

Mr Yunus was a man of many parts who had a penchant for wry humour. He would preside over the lengthy working sessions of the Committee members and often intervene with a witty remark or anecdote.

He was a close associate of Khan Abdul Gaffar Khan, also known as Frontier Gandhi and participated in national freedom movement with Pandit Jawahar Lal Nehru.

Prime Minister Nehru inducted him in the Indian Foreign Service and he served as India's Ambassador to Turkey, Iran, Indonesia and Spain. Later he was appointed as Chairman, Trade Fair Authority of India in the rank of a Minister of the Central Government.

Among the numerous anecdotes with which Mr Yunus regaled the members of National Committee on Tourism and lightened the atmosphere amidst lengthy discussions, following are worth mentioning.

Mr R K NEHRU, ICS, FOREIGN SECRETARY

Mr R K Nehru, Foreign Secretary of India, an ICS well known for his vast scholarship, entered Prime Minister Nehru's office to tender his resignation from service. On Prime Minister Nehru's asking for his reasons for resigning, he mentioned having been grossly offended by Mohammad Yunus, then a Deputy Secretary but known to be a very close associate of Prime Minister Nehru. He went on to add that Yunus had the gumption to call him a "bloody fool".

Prime Minister Nehru immediately summoned Mr Yunus and severely admonished him for his insolence and directed him to apologise to the Foreign Secretary, which Mr Yunus did rather angrily and left.

Mollified by the apology, Mr R K Nehru withdrew his resignation and returned to his office chamber.

A few minutes later, Mr Yunus, barged in to remonstrate with Prime Minister Nehru for having humiliated him so severely in front of the Foreign Secretary.

Prime Minister Nehru looked irritated for a moment and then said, to Mr Yunus that "you had no business to call the Foreign Secretary a bloody fool to his face what most people call him behind his back!"

Prime Minister Indira Gandhi's Directive

Mr Yunus related this story of a directive to him by Prime Minister Mrs Gandhi, to personally visit each of the 15 South American countries, meet their Ministers of Trade to invite participation by their countries in India's Trade Fairs.

He succeeded in persuading a few of the South America's bigger nations to agree to their countries participation in the Trade Fair Authority of India's annual exhibitions.

In Paraguay, he faced reluctance for participation on the ground that they produce no items suitable for trade with India. Mr Yunus had a cordial meeting with that country's Minister of Trade but could not persuade him to agree to his country's participation.

An exasperated Mr Yunus told the Minister that he has been given a mandate by Prime Minister Mrs Gandhi to invite his country to participate. He will therefore not leave without his confirmation of his country accepting the invitation. The Paraguay Minister then said, Mr Yunus you are welcome to stay in our country as long as you like and expressed his good wishes for his enjoyable stay.

Mr Yunus replied to the Minister, that he had misunderstood him. "I did not say I will not go from your country. I meant that I will not leave your room and not let you leave it till you agree." The Minister of Trade of Paraguay then yielded and agreed to have a few of their items sent for display in the exhibition at New Delhi.

30

PATA Gold Award Grand Category: 1990

Pacific Asia Tourism Association (PATA), a global organisation was founded in 1957 at San Francisco for providing responsible and insightful research for development of travel and tourism. Its membership comprised of 95 Government, State and Tourism bodies, 25 international airlines, 108 hospitality organisations and 72 educational institutions.

PATA has an annual scheme of presenting PATA Gold Awards for exceptional achievements in four principal categories: Marketing, Heritage and Culture, Tourism Education and Training and Environment. These awards are presented to the winners at its Annual Sessions which are organised in member-countries.

In 1987, the Ministry of Tourism appointed me as the head of the newly founded Indian Institute of Tourism and Travel Management (IITTM) tasked to develop it as the National Centre of Excellence for Tourism training.

This entailed establishing linkage with leading Universities in India and abroad and setting up Regional Centres of the Institute in the States.

In 1990, I authored a comprehensive compendium of Tourism curricula comprising of Management development programmes, Training of Trainer programmes and the post graduate degree course of Master of Tourism Administration (MTA) which has been adopted by a large number of Universities in India and South Asia.

It transpired that in 1990, PATA instituted the Gold Award Grand Category for exceptional achievement in the field of tourism education, and invited entries for the award from member organisations.

The Ministry of Tourism, Government of India decided to enter my name for the award of the PATA's first Gold Award Grand in recognition of my contributions to the human resource development of tourism sector in India and the South Asian Countries.

31

'Paan' at the Indian Banquet at Islamabad

Following the 1965 Indo-Pak war, the diplomatic relations between the two countries remained suspended for the next 10 years, resulting in total breakdown of trade between the two countries.

In December 1974, a Pakistan trade delegation visited India to explore the possibilities of resumption of trade. The Government of India decided to reciprocate by sending an Indian trade delegation in January, 1975, led by Mr Y T Shah, the then Secretary of Ministry of Commerce. The delegation included representatives of the Ministries of External Affairs, Industry, Food and Agriculture, Home and Economic Affairs.

I was then working as Director Foreign Trade, South Asia Division, Ministry of Commerce and was included as a member of the Indian Trade Delegation.

Mr Y T Shah, the leader of the Indian delegation, held two preparatory meetings of the members and defined their respective role and responsibilities during the trade talks at Islamabad.

I was assigned the task of collecting from each member the offer list of items of their respective Ministries available for export to Pakistan.

Their respective offer lists were discussed and cleared at the next preparatory meeting chaired by Mr Y T Shah. The total number of Indian goods on offer for export were over 200.

Mr Y T Shah advised the representative of Ministry of Food and Agriculture to have the Indian *Paan* (Betel leaf) added to his Ministry's List of export items. He explained that *Paan*, an after meal- treat of both poor and rich, was a popular item of Indian export prior to the 1965 war. It would be welcomed by all the people of Pakistan.

I was advised to arrange the best quality of *Paan* packed and taken with the delegation for serving at the traditional banquet to be hosted by the leader of the Indian delegation on conclusion of the 3-day trade talks in Islamabad.

The representative of the Ministry of External Affairs was assigned the responsibility of liaising with the Embassy of Switzerland, which was looking after India's interest in the absence of an Indian Embassy during the period of breakdown of diplomatic relations between India and Pakistan for any facilities or assistance that may be required by the Indian Delegation during their stay in Pakistan.

The Delegation landed at Islamabad on 19th January 1975 and was welcomed by the Leader of the Pakistan Delegation. Mr Ejaz Ahmed Naik, Commerce Secretary of Pakistan.

WELCOME AT ISLAMABAD AIRPORT

Talks commenced next day and were held in a cordial atmosphere. The only hiatus was, while the Indian offer list included 200 items for export to Pakistan, that country had a much smaller list.

At the request of the Pakistan delegation, the Indian offer list had to be pruned as it could have had serious political implications in Pakistan.

The leader of the Pakistan delegation, Mr Ejaz Ahmed Naik hosted a dinner in honour of the Indian delegation on 21st January 1975. In his speech, Mr Naik remarked that the name of the leader of the Indian delegation, (Shah) could well be the name of the leader of the Pakistan delegation, while his (Naik) could well be the name of the leader of Indian delegation! The quip made it to the front pages of Pakistan media the next day.

32

Auditing Accounts of Prime Minister's House

I learnt this amazing story of a new entrant to the Indian Audit and Accounts Service in the 60's being required to carry out an independent audit of the accounts of Prime Minister Jawahar Lal Nehru's official residence, Teenmurti House from an esteemed colleague of the Audit and Accounts Service.

A young probationer in the 60's, (name withheld to avoid hurting sentiments of family members), was assigned to carry out the audit of the accounts of Teenmurti House, the official residence of India's first Prime Minister, Jawahar Lal Nehru.

Nehru was an immensely popular world leader. During his long tenure as Prime Minister, Teenmurti House played host to several global leaders, celebrities and dignitaries. Many of them stayed there to be able to spend more time with Nehru. The official expenditure on hosting these visits at Teenmurti House was considerable.

The IA&AS probationer and his team of auditors were provided full access to the accounts. They went through the accounts with a fine tooth comb but, much to their disappointment, found them meticulously maintained without any flaw which could be included in his report of the audit.

The PM House staff sensing the probationer's disappointment suggested that he take his team of auditors on a tour of the beautifully manicured gardens of Teenmurti House, accompanied by the Garden Superintendent. This functionary took great pride in his maintenance of the extremely well-tended gardens, a much favoured area of Pandit Nehru for his morning walks and yoga asanas.

The disappointed probationer was hardly paying any attention to the Garden Superintendent's running commentary when he suddenly spotted trees laden with a variety of fruit. His eyes lit up at this discovery. He tactfully enquired about the disposal of the fruits grown on a public property, by Government staff, with official resources. The Garden Superintendent gleefully informed him that Pandit Nehru was very fond of fruit and relished them at his breakfast.

The probationer's next question as to who paid for them, shocked the poor man. Aghast, he reacted, somewhat sternly, that there can be no question of the Prime Minister paying for consuming fruit grown in his own garden.

The probationer heaved a sigh of relief. He had achieved what he set out to do. He had found the illusive misuse worth reporting to his superiors. He carefully counted the number of fruit laden trees, estimated the quantity of fruit grown on each and calculated the loss sustained by the Exchequer owing to non-payment of the cost of fruit that would have been served for the Prime Minister's breakfast. He returned to his Headquarters quite pleased with his performance and submitted the report of his first independent audit check. For added effect, he recommended that the dues for the fruit consumed be recovered from the staff responsible for this lapse in the Prime Minister's House.

His immediate superior to whom the report was submitted was stunned by the thoughtlessness of the probationer and 'put up' the report to the next senior, the Dy. CAG, with the remark that "the young officer is inexperienced and would be suitably advised to be more careful in future".

The Dy. CAG, equally irritated by the audacity of the probationer, endorsed the report to the big boss, the CAG, with the observation that "the probationer will be cautioned to exercise discretion in such sensitive cases in future". They waited with bated breath for the CAG's reaction, which came as an absolute shocker. The CAG had simply minuted: "I agree with the probationer's findings".

The astonished hierarchy in the CAG's office had no option, but to forward the Probationer's Audit report, with the CAG's observation, to the Prime Minister's Secretary, then, an ICS officer. He was irritated by the thoughtlessness of the young Audit officer and decided to let the Prime Minister see and decide for himself. The file remained on the Prime Minister's desk for a day or two, and when it came back, there was a bigger surprise waiting for them, Prime Minister Nehru had pinned his personal cheque for Rs 5000 for the fruit consumed by him.

The message from the nation's Founding Father was loud and clear "Institutions are more important than individuals".

33

Montgomery's Drumbeat at the Yacht Club

The Bombay Yacht Club and the Delhi Gymkhana Club have a reciprocal agreement to provide accommodation for their respective members during their visits.

During my stay there as a member of the Delhi Gymkhana Club, I came across a fascinating tale in the "Memoirs of Field Marshal Bernard L. Montgomery", of his experience of staying at the Royal Yacht Club, as it was known then, in 1903. It makes interesting reading :

> "While in Bombay along with two other subalterns, was invited to a dinner party by a senior British officer of our battalion, Captain R. Wood. Being an old and staid Captain, he went home early and left the three Subalterns to continue their party at the Club".

Next morning the senior of the three Subalterns received the following letter from the Secretary of the Club:

"It has been reported to me by several members of the Club that last evening after dinner you and your friends behaved in a most ungentlemanly and uproarious way in the bar of the Royal Bombay Yacht Club between the hours of 10:30 p.m. and 2:00 a.m., shouting loudly, beating the brass topped bar tables and drumming on them. This conduct caused great annoyance and disgust to members who were playing billiards and to other members playing cards upstairs. I am informed that your shouts and cries and drumming could be heard all over the club building. When the Hall Porter of the Club went to you, pointing out the rule which prohibits such disgraceful and unseemly proceedings in the Club, you apparently paid no attention to him but continued as before. The Hall Porter then reported to me. I arrived to find that the officers concerned had left and the disturbance had, for the time, ceased".

"I have to refer you to by-Law VII which you have broken. The occurrence will be reported to the Committee of the Club and will be dealt with. The officer chiefly concerned in the uproarious proceedings, in addition to yourself, was Lieutenant B L Montgomery".

Needless to mention that the young subaltern was later to become Field Marshal Lord Montgomery who led the Eighth Army's famed 2000 miles long march from Alamein through Libya, Tunis, Sicily, Italy, France and Germany to the shores of the Baltic sea, demolishing the Panzer divisions of Field Marshal Rommel, taking 248,000 prisoners of war and taking the surrender of the German Northern Armies at Luneburg Heath on 4th May 1945, bringing the Second World War to an end.

Montgomery was known for his austere food preferences. He was a vegetarian and a teetotaller. King George-VI, accompanied by Winston Churchill, is said to have visited Montgomery's field Headquarters in Europe during the Second World War. He is reported to have offered the monarch sandwiches and tea.

On 4th May 1945, Field Marshal Montgomery accepted the unconditional surrender of the German forces at Luneburg Heath, near Hamburg from Admiral Friedeburg Commander-in-Chief of the German Navy and General Kinzel of the German Army. After the surrender ceremony, Field Marshal Montgomery invited the German Admiral and General for dinner in his tent.

Montgomery's act of entertaining the defeated German General and Admiral in his tent raised a furore in the British Parliament. Churchill had to rise to ask: How many of the Hon'ble members have had the pleasure of enjoying the hospitality of Field Marshal Montgomery. When none responded, he added: ***"I have had that pleasure and assure you my sympathies are with the German Generals"***. The House dissolved in laughter and the issue was resolved.

Monty is said to have been asked by a well known columnist to name three greatest Generals of the world. He is said to have responded ***"the other two were Alexander and Napoleon".***

BLUE BOX CAFE

In November 2017 Tiffany's opened a restaurant on the 4th Floor called **"Blue Box Cafe"** which serves a US $ 40 Breakfast.

PART - IV
Memories of Mandvi

36

Memories of Mandvi

I was born at Kutch-Mandvi on 13th September 1938. I left the town in my infancy with my parents for Jodhpur, my home town.

I have no memories of my birthplace as circumstances never so transpired that I return to Mandvi.

My only recollections of Mandvi were the annual birthday gift of Mandvi Sweets which the Indian postal system meticulously delivered at my Jodhpur home on that date, an event, I eagerly looked forward to each year.

My recollections of Mandvi were, however, rekindled regularly by the visits of my four maternal uncles with their families to Jodhpur showering me with their affections and gifts.

One of my maternal uncles, Mr Vishram Puri, a qualified Civil Engineer, was appointed as Executive Engineer, Public Works Department (PWD) Jodhpur State and later moved to Jaipur, the capital of Rajasthan. He would be a permanent link to my birthplace and kept me up-to-date with news of my maternal family.

My eldest maternal uncle Mr Lal Puri was a Representative cum Distributor for the Times of India in Kutch - Mandvi and had his office on Bunder Road of in town.

He was the Santa Claus who never forgot my birthdays and his affectionate gift would invariably reach me, well in time, wherever I happened to be.

Being a regular reader of the Times of India, a few years ago I had a pleasant surprise waiting for me in its issue of 1st June 2007 on the edit page which I am reproducing below ad verbatim:

Times of India, New Delhi, 1st June 2007
Memories of TOI
DILIP JOSHI

"My first recollection of reading a daily is that of Times of India. It was sometime in the late 50s in Mandvi, a sleepy town in Kutch. A few hundred feet from where we lived was the office of the newspaper/magazine distributors known as Puri Brothers. The owner was a pleasingly plump gentleman in his fifties whom everybody called Lalpuri Sahib".

"In those days there was no Gujarat editions. The paper used to come all the way from Mumbai. There was an Indian Airline flight operating thrice a week across the Bombay-Bhavnagar-Jamnagar-Bhuj route. Many time it used to get cancelled and we would receive TOI in bunches."

"Lal Puri Sahib also represented TOI as their Reporter. I remember him occupying a prominent seat at most of the important functions that took place in Mandvi. Because of his size, he could not squat on the floor as was the norm those days. He would demand a chair which would be duly provided, thanks to his TOI connection, after which he would position himself at a vantage point with a pad and pen in hand."

"Memories of TOI' reminiscences of my maternal uncle Lal Puri Sahib turned "Memories of Mandvi" for me and have stayed that way.

My foremost memory of Mandvi was shared with me by my father. He described my journey as an infant in the loving arms of my mother, along with him to Karachi on board a passenger ship from Kutch enroute to Jodhpur. During the two day halt at Karachi, the family stayed at the mansion of a Marwari businessman, Mr Shiv Charan Mohta. He had a thriving business of export of red stone to England and other countries of Europe.

My father would often describe the grand style in which Mohta had built the mansion for his residence on the famous Clifton Beach of Karachi. He advised me to visit it, whenever, I had the opportunity to go to Karachi.

I had this opportunity three and a half decades later, during a brief halt at Karachi airport en-route to New Delhi to fulfil his desire and complete my memories of Mandvi.

37

Vignettes

Bouquet For Prakash Tandon

Prakash Tandon was a legendary business leader who became the first Indian Chairman of Hindustan Lever Limited in 1961, the first national of a developing country to become the Chairman of a Unilever subsidiary.

His closest associate at the Hindustan Lever was Vice - Chairman Maurice Zinkin, a retired British Civil Servant. His wife Taya Zinkin was a renowned journalist who represented the Guardian in India and authored the famous books *"Reporting India"* and *"India Changes"*.

The author (centre) with Mr N G Goray (left) and Mr Maurice Zinkin (right)

The author (left) with Mr Prakash Tandon (right)

I had my first exposure to them in London during my tenure as Director, India Tea Promotion from 1977 to 1980 when Prakash Tandon led a high level Tea Enquiry Committee to survey the prospects for boosting the exports of Indian tea to England, Europe and USA.

My office located on Oxford Street, at its junction with Bond Street, known as India Tea Centre, became the venue for the team's meetings with the representatives of British Tea Trade.

Mr Prakash Tandon, Mr Maurice Zinkin and his wife Taya Zinkin attended the receptions I used to host from time to time at the India Tea Centre.

After the meetings were over, Mr Tandon would invariably utilise the facilities attached to my office. I noticed that he would carry his shaver to spruce up for his evening engagements and request for a caddy of Indian tea for his hosts of the evening.

During that period, we had received a few of the highest quality of tea caddies from the Tea Board of India for presentation to Her Majesty the Queen of England for seeking recognition of "By Appointment to the Queen".

Mr Tandon asked me if he could take a special caddy as a gift to his hosts of the evening, Mr David Orr, who was Chairman of the Unilever Company in London and his wife Lady Orr.

I decided to play a jest on Mr Tandon, by telling him that Mr David Orr as Vice Chairman of Hindustan Lever Ltd. had interviewed me for a post of an Executive and had not deemed me suitable for it. Therefore, no tea caddy for him.

Mr Tandon seemed nonplussed for a moment and then recovered his poise saying I understand. I promptly put him at his ease, apologised for the teaser and handed him a beautifully gift-wrapped Caddy of Tea for Mr and Mrs Orr.

The next morning when he came to my office, he told me that Lady Orr was delighted with the gift, and then asked me to guess what he had said to Mr David Orr?

Sensing my reluctance to hazard a guess, Mr Tandon said I told David that the gift is by courtesy of someone you did not consider suitable for Hindustan Lever and added that the "the loss of Hindustan Lever Ltd. has been the gain of Tea Board of India".

I had the honour of meeting Mr Prakash Tandon numerous times on my return to India and had many more opportunities of learning from his vast experience and abilities as an outstanding writer.

THE BUG LETTER

Mr Ranjit Singh, a high ranking officer of Indian Railways in the post-independence era headed the Commercial Department of the Northern Railway.

I was assigned to his office during my training phase as an Assistant Traffic Superintendent (ATS) of the Indian Railway Traffic Service in 1962 – 63.

I found in Mr Singh an extremely suave and considerate superior who would often share with me his experiences of travels on foreign railways in Europe, America and Afro-Asian Continents under a protocol of the International Union of Railways based in Paris, under which officers of member Railways could avail facilities of complimentary travel on their respective railway systems.

I recall an amusing story of Mr Singh's experience of travel on one of America's most popular tourist trains, the Amtrak Coast which starts it's journey from Seattle and culminates at Los Angles.

Mr Singh had booked a twin sleeping coupe for himself and his wife, almost an year in advance. The President of Amtrak had replied to Mr Singh, welcoming him and assuring of special arrangements for his travel on the Amtrak during his visit.

Mr Singh's experience however, turned out to be rather unpleasant. Their overnight journey in a twin bed sleeper was uncomfortable and their sleep disturbed by bed bugs in the coupe !. Their complaint to the coach attendant yielded no relief.

Now comes the hilarious part. On return to India, Mr Singh wrote to the President of Amtrak apprising him of his plight on board the country's most popular tourist train.

He received a response almost a month later. The letter printed on an embossed letter head of the President, Amtrak, was most edifying. Its contents read:

"Amtrak's enquiry on your complaint have revealed gross negligence on the part of the concerned train attendants. They have been suitably punished. We assure you that in future when any officer of your rank travels, special facilities would be provided to ensure their visit offers them the best of comforts and a memorable experience".

Mr Singh decided to save the letter for future use if required and was putting it back in the envelope when a small card slipped out of the envelope. On it was marked in the handwriting of the President, the instruction: SEND THIS GUY THE BUG LETTER!

I am Domecq

This is my story .... Like Romeo and Juliet, I commemorate the unrequited love of John Ruskin, England's most famous romantic poet for a rich Spanish Heiress Adele - Clothide Domecq who went on to marry for fame and fortune, Seigneur Féodal, a Frenchman.

The poet John Ruskin retired hurt in love to his home 'Brentwood' on Coniston Lake, Cumbria.

As their homage to the failed relationship of John Ruskin with their daughter Adele, her parents created me, 'Domecq Sherry', a gift for the poet.

The Domecq family has maintained this tradition by exclusively creating 'Domecq Sherry' for distribution to the guests at Brentwood.

In April 1978, I was presented to Mr R. K. Puri, Director of Tea Board of India who organised tea promotions in Lake District hotels and visited 'Brentwood'.

I have adorned the glass cabinet at his home in New Delhi India all these years.

This is my autobiography.

Toast to Mr Sahay

Mr P. Sahay was the General Manager of Northern Railway in 1962 when I joined the Indian Railway Traffic Service on that Railway.

We soon learnt that Mr Sahay was due to be elevated as a Member of the Railway Board and prior to that would be attending a three-month exchange programme of Top Executives of Railways of various countries.

As the date of his departure arrived near, a function was organised at the Railway Officers Club to bid farewell to Mr Sahay. All officers were invited to the function.

Prior to the arrival of the Chief Guest, the organiser of the function, a senior officer made some announcements regarding the programme of the evening. He especially enjoined all officers to rise with the glasses filled with a soft drink to join him in proposing a toast to Mr Sahay.

The practice of raising toasts to bid farewell to a colleague which was prevalent in the British era has become extinct after independence.

The invitees found the proposal rather odd but followed the drill prescribed as the organiser welcomed Mr Sahay, briefly explained the purpose of his visit to USA and invited us to join him in raising a toast to Mr Sahay. He then added "may he come back with new ideas for the betterment of Indian Railways".

Before the guests could raise their glasses, Mr Sahay intervened with an amendment to the toast:

"Ladies and Gentlemen, at my age it is rather difficult to acquire new ideas. I have always believed that Indian Railways have a lot to share with Railways of other countries. It is in that spirit I am going to USA. Raise your glasses with me".

VICEREINE THE ADC

Lady Willingdon, Vicereine of India, is credited with having raised the fund for constructing a swimming pool at the Gymkhana Club, New Delhi known as the "Lady Willingdon Swimming Bath".

At a formal dinner hosted by the Viceroy Lord Willingdon at the Government House, the ADC on the duty of the Vicereine was listening to an animated conversation among the lady guests about the strange titles being given to the dance tunes of that era, a subject in which he had considerable expertise. He piped in with the name of a dance tune titled "I shall remember your kisses when you have forgotten my name".

The Vicereine, Lady Willingdon was listening to another conversation at one end of the table and did not hear what had been said by the ADC and invited him to repeat his remark.

Sensing that something profound was about to be said, all talk ceased and all eyes turned to the ADC. Somewhat flustered by this attention, he murmured shyly "I will remember Your Kisses, Your Excellency when you have forgotten my name".

The silence that followed could have been broken by a pin falling.

SIR HARCOURT BUTLER'S RIPOSTE

Sir Harcourt Butler is a well known name in North Indian Schools in Shimla and Delhi bear his name. He was the first President of Delhi Gymkhana Club, New Delhi.

He was also known for his skills as an outstanding speaker, especially in proposing toasts at formal banquets held to commemorate the King and Queen's birthdays or in welcoming the Viceroys and Governors presiding over the official banquets.

This was also the cause of arousing feelings of jealousy among his contemporaries in the Civil Services.

At one such banquet, presided by a Lieutenant Governor of a province, who wanted to know who was willing to propose the after dinner toast, none was willing.

He then turned to Sir Harcourt Butler and remarked that you are known for your skills as an orator. Your friends say that "Put up a dinner and you will come up with a speech".

Sir Harcourt delivered a brilliant after dinner speech and in conclusion thanked his colleague's remark about his skills as an orator and added that regrettably "When Your Excellency speaks, up comes my dinner".

The Liar King

George Nathaniel Curzon, Marquess of Kedleston was the Viceroy of India from 1899 to 1905.

He was an arrogant and haughty person who held a high opinion of his race as a white man.

Even while studying at Balliol College, Oxford, a doggerel about him in the college journal said:

"I am George Nathaniel
Curzon,
I am a most superior
person;
My face is pink, my hair is
black
I dine at Blenheim once
a week".

Curzon once called Indians a race of liars. This led to a political storm in India.

An enterprising journalist discovered that Curzon had falsely declared his age to be more than what it actually was when he learnt that Chinese have more respect for older people.

This encouraged an Urdu Shayar (Poet) of that era to coin this couplet for Curzon's lie:

"GAR HUM ZHOOTE
TO TUM ZHOOTON KE
BADSHAH".

Translated in English, it says:
"If we are liars,
you are the king of
liars"

Curzon once said famously that *"as long as we rule India, we are the greatest power in the world. If we lose it, we shall drop straightaway to a third rate power"*.

AMNESTY BIN

In 1995, during a three-week long tourism promotion tour covering cities in United Kingdom, USA, Australia and Philippines, my wife very thoughtfully packed a few Indian vegetarian snacks in my baggage as a safeguard against any pangs of starvation I may experience as a vegetarian in these countries.

Among other items in the baggage, there was also a longish list of items of gifts for friends and relatives to be brought by me. I could notice only one item demanded by my spouse –'Californian Almonds'.

During my journey through various European and British cities and onwards through the USA, the packets of vegetarian snacks that she had packed came in very handy. I blessed the spouse for her thoughtfulness.

In the hustle and bustle of foreign cities, I forgot to pick up the Californian Almonds till I saw them displayed at San Francisco International Airport. I immediately picked them up and put them in my briefcase. I boarded the Quantas direct flight to Sydney International Airport.

During the 15-hour non-stop Quantas flight from San Francisco to Sydney, there were frequent announcements that 'Australia is a germ free country and to keep it that way, passengers are not allowed to carry any food items. If they had any, those can be dropped in the Amnesty Box kept in the cabin service area.

At the Sydney airport near the Customs check-in counter a large Amnesty Box was placed where the arriving passengers could be seen discarding their items of snacks, biscuits, wafers, chocolates, etc., which they were carrying in their handbags or in their pockets.

As the vegetarian snacks carried by me were in my check-in baggage, I decided to declare them at the Customs check-in counter.

On reaching the counter, the lady manning the customs counter asked me what do I have to declare? I explained to her that being a vegetarian, I do carry some dry snack packets.

The Customs lady officer desired to see them. I opened my briefcase to pull out the beautifully gift wrapped Californian Almonds packet.

Recognising the item, the customs Lady officer smiled and saying "Oh these are of no problem, you may go", she waived me through.

It saved me considerable embarrassment as while going out I noticed that an Australian TV team was making a documentary on the Customs Check-ins in progress at the Sydney Airport. I was spared having to display Haldiram's or Bikanerwala's savouries on the customs counter being filmed for a TV documentary.

It earned me a warm thank you from my better half who was pleased to receive her choice item of Californian Almonds.

A Much Married Ambassador

An Indian Ambassador of royal lineage had gained a reputation of being of a romantic disposition, having divorced two wives and married a third one, younger to him by almost half his age and of exceptional beauty.

The Ambassador and his third wife were hosting the Indian National Day reception in a South Asian country.

The Ambassador was engaged in conversation with a Minister of that country who was the Chief Guest at the reception leaving his wife in the company of the Embassy's First Secretary.

The Ambassador's wife drew a lot of attention from the guests who came forward to talk to her. The Indian First Secretary was busy introducing the guests to the Ambassador's wife.

A young diplomat from a western country came forward to be introduced to the charming hostess of the evening.

As the Indian First Secretary was introducing the young diplomat to the lady, the latter in his excitement of greeting her, said "Oh I know her, she is the daughter of His Excellency the Indian Ambassador".

Her Excellency was by then on her third Margarita and with an amused look in her eyes as she corrected the western diplomat by introducing herself, saying

> "No, No, I am not the
> daughter of the Indian
> Ambassador. How can such
> an ugly fellow have so
> beautiful a daughter. I am
> his wife".

All conversation ceased. The western the diplomat didn't know where to disappear.

THE ASTERICK PULLED THE TRICK

President Zakir Hussain was on a State visit to Malaysia. His itinerary included a visit to Sarawak, a picturesque Malaysian state along the islands northwest coast including many beaches and historic landmarks.

The Presidential party consisting of the Minister on Duty, His Secretary, ADCs, Doctor and personal staff. The accompanying press party consisted of about 20 persons.

The list of accompanying persons showing their names, status in protocol, food preference etc. was faxed to the Governor of Sarawak two days in advance to enable the hosts to make arrangement for their stay.

Here, a hilarious but unintended *faux-pas* occurred. The Lady Secretary who faxed the list of members of the Presidential entourage was asked to put an asterisk against the name of the President's Doctor to denote his food preference as vegetarian.

While transmitting the names of the Presidential entourage to the Governor of Sarawak, the lady typist got confused on seeing two asterisks', one prefixed to the name at the top of list as Dr. Zakir Hussain, the other at the bottom of the list as Dr. (Physician).

The confused typist inadvertently put the asterisk against the name of the President.

This sent the Governor of Sarawak's office in a frenzy. They had planned the entire menu for the Presidential Banquet with choicest non-vegetarian dishes.

Now, at the last minute, they were required to switch to a vegetarian menu for which they had neither a chef nor the ingredients.

The net result: An Indian Vegetarian Chef from Bangkok was flown to Kuching, the capital city of Sarawak.

The next day's banquet held in honour of the visiting President of India was unique and extra-ordinary.

The banquet table was laden with fancy vegetarian dishes and few non-vegetarian dishes which were placed discreetly away from the President.

The gentle Dr. Zakir Hussain gave no indication of him not being served the food of his preference and expressed his profound appreciation to the Governor of Sarawak and his team of officers for their excellent hospitality and courtesy extended to him making it a memorable visit.

Later on in the evening on seeing his Physician, he smilingly enquired how he enjoyed the feast at the Banquet.

THREE IN ONE

Travellers Club London, located at 106 Pall Mall, near the Trafalgar Square is known as one of the oldest gentleman's clubs in London.

It had reciprocal arrangements with clubs in 140 countries including the Delhi Gymkhana Club and was my favourite place to stay during visits to London.

On one visit, while staying there, I was invited to lunch at the Travellers by an old friend, Alban Davis. He had also invited a few other friends to join us for lunch. The Dining Hall was fully packed with members and their guests. During the lunch, an elderly club member entered the dining hall and seemed to know a large number of diners as he went around shaking hands. An invitee of Alban, he was soon seated at our table. As he approached our table, Alban introduced him to all of us as 'Edwin'. It rang no bell for me.

Edwin soon had the guests in splits with his repartees and witty remarks. Post lunch as goodbyes were bid, he kissed the lady seated next to him, thanked Alban and took his leave. The solitary lady guest at our table enquired after the guest from Alban, as he had ensured an afternoon of laughter with his witty remarks. Alban shared that the guest who had been seated next to her was the President of the Travellers Club and known as Field Marshal Edwin Noel Bramall, Baron and former Chief of the British Defence Staff and all land forces.

The vivacious lady gasped and remarked that this was the first time in her life that she had been kissed by somebody who is *'three in one'* - President of a Club, a Field Marshal and a Baron of the British realm.

38

Father, Friend, Philosopher and Guide

My father, Mr Kishen Puri, a Senior Civil Servant of the Jodhpur state, was my friend, philosopher and guide and one of the most caring persons who filled a deep void in my life of losing my mother in my infancy.

He was helped in this task by my two widowed aunts, Ganga Devi and Sushila Devi, who nursed and brought me up with abundant love and affection as my fairy godmothers.

My father, despite his numerous official and social commitments, invariably devoted his evenings to me, educating me in his own subtle way, talking about historical figures, famous writers and poets, and would make me listen to news broadcasts from All India Radio, British Broadcasting Corporation and Voice of America. He would add a subtle touch of humour about the Broadcasters to arouse my interest.

I recall the names of the broadcasters I heard in childhood like A.S. Bokhari, and Z. A. Bokhari, of the All India Radio (AIR).

Father would smilingly add that the name AIR has been changed to BBC and with a glint in his eye explained, it means Bokhari Brothers Corporation. I have never forgotten the story.

He introduced me to the name of Dorothy Thompson, the lead newsreader of Voice of America and would add ***'What Dorthy speaks today, America will speak tomorrow'***.

I was 9 years old, studying in Class V at Jodhpur when father woke me up shortly before midnight on 14th August 1947 to listen to a historic broadcast on All India Radio.

For the first time I heard the never to be forgotten voice of India's first Prime Minister, Jawahar Lal Nehru deliver at the stroke of midnight on 14th August 1947 his historic "TRYST WITH DESTINY" speech regarded as one of the greatest speeches of the 20th Century.

He encouraged me to memorise this speech which I could recite et verbatim at the school and college functions later. It stayed in my memory till very recently as a great address. I could recite its opening paragraph even now:

"Long years ago we made a tryst with destiny and now the time comes when we shall redeem our pledge not wholly or in full measure, but very substantially. At the stroke of midnight hour when the world sleeps, India will awake to life and freedom: A moment comes, which comes once when an age ends, and when the soul of a nation .... "

It was a great learning phase in my childhood with a learned father sharing his vast knowledge with me as a scholar, author, speaker and administrator. His portfolio of top administrative positions held in the Jodhpur State covered almost all departments.

He had been Secretary, Department of Home, Industries, Judicial, Health, Law and Commerce, culminating as Chief Secretary, before the merger of the state in the Union of India.

He had also served as a Police Officer in the State, attaining the rank of a Deputy Inspector General of Police.

He authored a book titled the *"Memoirs of Marwar Police*", published in 1937 and widely acclaimed in the media reviews of that era as the only authoritative book of its kind on the police organisation in India.

Searching for the availability of copies of his book in 2021 on the internet 84 years after it was published in 1937, I was amazed to discover it in the Library of US Congress, Library of St. Pancras, London, Brown University and other Ivy league universities of USA.

My father who had held the portfolio of Law Secretary of the Jodhpur State planned a legal career for me and used to often tell me about the achievements of legal icons of that period. They included Mr M R Jayakar, Sir Tej Bahadur Sapru, Mr M C Setalvad, Mr Moti Lal Nehru, Mr MA Jinnah, Mr MC Chagla, Mr N Palkhiwala amongst other eminent counsels.

I learnt about the iconic legal figures of Britain, like Mr F E Smith who was later elevated as Earl of Birkenhead on becoming the Lord Chancellor of Justice of England.

I vividly recall the story of how F E Smith came to the rescue of a junior counsel who had been summoned by a Court to show cause why he should not be sentenced for contempt of Court.

The story goes that the young counsel was appearing in a case for which he had prepared himself as the defence attorney very thoroughly. Nevertheless, he lost the case and was walking out of the court dejectedly. The judge happened to pass him by and turning to the young lawyer asked him what he thought of the judgement.

The young lawyer replied rather dejectedly that "he was surprised by the judgement". Next day he was served notice for contempt of Court.

The terrified young lawyer rushed to the senior counsel Mr F E Smith and related his tale of woes, seeking his protection. Mr Smith moved by his plight agreed to defend him.

Senior Counsel F E Smith appeared on behalf of the young lawyer in the hearing of the contempt of Court proceedings on the due date.

The Judge who was aware of the high standing of Barrister F E Smith among the legal icons of England was suitably chastened by his appearance in his Court and heard the defence with rapt attention.

Barrister F E Smith completely demolished the case for contempt of Court and proved beyond doubt that no contempt had been committed by the young lawyer. Then came the punch line:

"My Lord, the young lawyer is inexperienced but had he my experience of your Lordship's judgements, he would never have been surprised at any of your Lordship's judgements."

The contempt proceedings ..... demolished.

I learnt at an early age about the four Inns of Court of England, which are known as:

(i) Inner Temple

(ii) Middle Temple

(iii) Lincoln's Temple and

(iv) Gray's Inn

Those aspiring for a legal Career as a Barrister have to join one of the above Inns of Court.

Father shared a limerick about the Inns with me which, I recall even now:

"Swells go to Inner Temple
Middlings to Middle Temple
Lawyers to Lincoln Temple
Paupers to the Gray's Inn"

Pandit Jawahar Lal Nehru went to the Inner Temple while Mahatma Gandhi qualified as a Barrister from Middle Temple.

To qualify as a Barrister-at-law, aspiring candidates are required to attend a certain number of formal dinners which are addressed by eminent Barristers. Exams are held in the Inns of Court where access to law books and journals is allowed for reference in the examinations. Those who quality are then called to the Bar.

Father had planned a course for me at the Middle Temple, coupled with a one year honours degree in Economics from the London School of Economics. He even took out a Foreign Education Insurance Policy for me to ensure no hitch arose in my undertaking this course of education.

The hitch did arise in terms of restrictions on release of foreign exchange for studies abroad in the early post-independence years. Instead, I went on to take a post graduate degree in Economics from the University of Rajasthan at 20 years of age in 1958.

This enabled me to appear in the All India Civil Services examination in 1960 and qualify for the Indian Police Service in 1961. I served for a year as a Probationary IPS Officer and was allotted to the Gujarat Cadre.

I took the Civil Service Examination again in 1961, as allowed under the Civil Service Rules, and qualified for appointment to the Traffic Transportation and Commercial Department of the Superior Revenue Establishment of Indian Railways (TT&CD) as the service was called during the British Rule in India and continued to be so called in the post-independence years till it was reconstituted as Indian Railway Traffic Service (IRTS) in 1967.

I joined the IRTS in 1962. It opened up new vistas of service in diverse and challenging sectors in the Government of India both within India and abroad, as already detailed in earlier chapters, till my retirement in 1996.

I was blessed to have the guidance of my Father till his demise in 1984.

Epilogue

As an octogenarian I recall my career of close to sixty years coming full circle from the initial two years in Corporate enterprises, to thirty-four years in the various Ministries of the Government of India, to the final twenty three years, as the founder Secretary General of the Hotel Association of India (HAI).

I had planned to appear in the All India Civil Service examination after my completion of Post-Graduation in Economics in 1958 from the University of Rajasthan but had to wait a year to attain the age of 21 years for appearing in the examination.

Two of the then top corporate houses of India became my learning ground. My first appointment was at a Birla enterprise as a Public Relations Officer at Jaipur.

The Company had a collaboration with a British Company, Hoffman and Co. whose representative, Mr Hambleton was Senior Technical Advisor of the Nation Engineering Industries, Jaipur. I was assigned to work with him.

Among the distinguished visitors to the Company whose programme of meetings with the senior management officers and visits to the plants I had to co-ordinate, were Mr George David Woods, President of the World Bank and the veteran industry leader, Mr Purshottamdas Thakurdas, signatory to the famous Bombay Plan of 1944, along with the other signatories: JRD Tata, AD Birla, John Mathai and few other members.

The Bombay Plan of 1944 was formulated by them for the post-independence development of Indian economy and regarded by experts as the precursor of India's First Five Year Plan.

George Woods, a close associate of Mr G D Birla, was a distinguished American Banker who is credited to have transformed the World Bank from a passive investment organisation into an active leader of world development.

Meeting these leaders of the finance world like Mr Purshottamdas Thakurdas and Mr George Wood was an inspiring learning experience for me at an early stage of my career.

I, however, did not foresee a long term career for myself in an engineering organisation and chose to opt out on completion of a year's probation period.

The New India Assurance Co. Bombay (now Mumbai), a Tata Group enterprise, floated a scheme for selection of executives to work overseas and invited applications from post graduates with an economics background for recruitment, to serve in their numerous offices.

I was selected for a year's training in Bombay before being posted abroad. I completed the major part of the training programme when the trainees were required to execute agreements to serve abroad for a period of 15 years. I had then recently got married and both of us, my wife and I did not wish to stay away from the country for a long period.

I then appeared in the All India Civil Service Examination in 1960 and qualified for appointment to the Indian Police Service - 1961, marking the commencement of my career of 34 years' service in the Government of India in multifarious capacities in various Ministries, Public Sector Organisations, UN assignments and heading the Tea Board of India, London as shared in the book.

The penultimate turn of my career wheel orchestrated my return to the Private Sector as the Secretary General of the Hotel Association of India from 1996 to 2020.

I chose to step down in June 2020. These 23 years could perhaps be a subject of another book.

Index

C

D

E

F

K

L

M

Q

R

W

Y

Z